SOCIAL SURVIVAL HANDBOOK

SOCIAL SURVIVAL HANDBOOK

Guy Browning

Illustrated by
Simon Torrance

SIMON & SCHUSTER

LONDON·SYDNEY·NEW YORK·TOKYO·SINGAPORE·TORONTO

First published in Great Britain by Simon & Schuster Ltd, 1994
A Paramount Communications Company
Copyright © Guy Browning, 1993

Simon & Schuster Ltd
West Garden Place
Kendal Street
London W2 2AQ

Simon & Schuster of Australia Pty Ltd
Sydney

A CIP catalogue record for this book is available from the
British Library.

ISBN 0–671 85239–6

Illustrated by Simon Torrance

Typeset in Sabon and Gill Sans

Printed in Great Britain

To my Mum and Dad

ACKNOWLEDGEMENTS

My thanks to Beth Wood, Jo Frank, Fenella Smart, Aruna Mathur, Jo Saker, Anna Powell, Alex Stitt, Julian Alexander, Deborah Orr, Roger Alton, Lorna Dolan, the Petley Road Ladies and Birgitta Meyer without whom this book would be a thin technical manual on sludge pump operation.

CONTENTS

DINNER PARTIES

D inner parties are the Himalayas of social life; 90% of all social activity and 35% of fatal social accidents take place at dinner parties, so getting them right is critical. The thing you have to remember about dinner parties is that they're not dinners and they're not parties; they're three hours attempting to communicate with alien life forms with your mouth full.

Getting the bottle to go

The only difference between dinner parties and death is that with dinner parties you can take something with you and that something is usually a bottle of wine. The wine you take is in effect a bottled character reference, so a little care is required.

There are only two types of wine: those that feature a 99p at the end of their price tag, and those that don't. Unless money is something you're keen to get rid of, get the second cheapest wine in the off-licence. Steer clear of the cheapest as this will be a *'wine-style beverage'* extracted from something other than grapes, such as petroleum jelly or Semtex.

REMEMBER: *The second cheapest wine is always £2.99. Keep the penny change to scrape the price tag off, but be careful that you don't uncover another price tag that says £1.99.*

If you feel that the wine you've bought amounts to a bottled slap in the face, get the off-licence to wrap it tightly in tissue paper. For some reason this makes it look more expensive. Once you've given the bottle to your host, check to see if they're impressed. If they whisk it away for private consumption, they are. If they pour it into an old tin and put dirty paintbrushes in it, they're not.

---

5 COUNTRIES WHOSE WINES HAVE NEVER APPEARED IN

SAINSBURY'S WINE DEPARTMENT TOP 10

(and aren't likely to for some considerable time yet)

1 Panama	3 Abu Dhabi	5 Scotland
2 Chad	4 French Guyana	

If you're offered wine from any of these countries, immediately extinguish all cigarettes, return to your seat and assume the brace position.

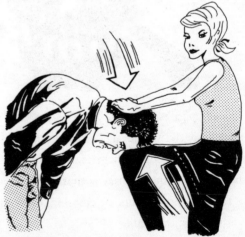

Wines from Chad are rarely appreciated

Don't come too soon

7.30 for 8 means 9.30 for 8. If you turn up at 7.30 you can expect to find your host still in his or her curlers, putting the finishing touches to a Pavlova with a blowtorch and a tube of Superglue.

Arriving at 9.30 also means that you don't run out of things to say by five past eight. If you've prepared a sparkling conversational gem guaranteed to set the evening alight, don't waste it. There's no point stepping through the door, blurting out, '*A first rate pizza is better than a second rate opera*' and then sitting like a lemon for the rest of the evening.

I'm allergic to anything from the Bodyshop

REMEMBER: *The trick is to turn up after all the other guests have arrived but before they sit down for the food. This gives the useful impression that when they eat is determined by when you arrive.*

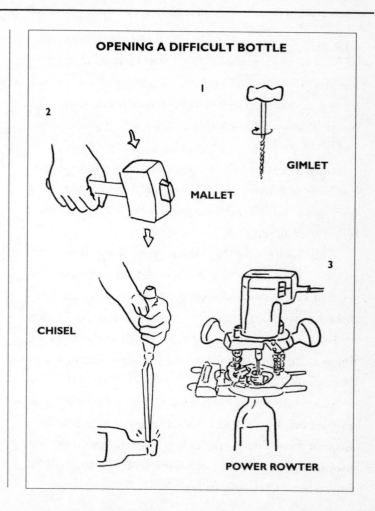

OPENING A DIFFICULT BOTTLE

GIMLET

MALLET

CHISEL

POWER ROWTER

Kissing

R esearch has found that the average man does more kissing at a dinner party than he does in a year's foreplay. Obviously it's not the same sort of kissing and it's not advisable to step through the door and drop your tongue down your host's throat. Especially if you've never met.

If you listen carefully to the tone of your host's greeting you'll know when a kiss is appropriate. *'Don't just stand there, gorgeous, kiss me!'* is a green light. *'Can I help you?'* is an amber at best.

With kissing, the key thing is to keep your neck relaxed. This allows for a rapid response if you find yourself in one of those kissing marathons involving two, three or even four kisses. It's very embarrassing for the host if after the kiss on the right cheek she's swooping round for another on the left and you're wandering off to find a drink.

Make sure you're clear of the front door when you start kissing. If you're not, another guest is bound to fling open the front door at the crucial moment, throwing you into the coat stand and forcing you to break your fall by ripping out a small light fitting.

REMEMBER: *Never kiss other people while they're talking or attempting to put food in their mouth.*

Getting introduced

I ntroductions are the most important five seconds of any dinner party. This is when people scrutinise you minutely and make snap judgements that will be set in stone despite anything you do or say for the rest of your life. At this stage therefore, do your best to look attractive and interesting. If you're not naturally attractive try and look especially interesting. If you're neither attractive nor interesting, go home.

The worst possible nightmare is when nobody introduces you. When this happens you feel like the losing candidate at the announcement of a by-election result; technically you exist but no one is quite able to speak to you.

Obviously the person to sit next to at a dinner party is the witty, charming and attractive one. You'll know this person because when you actually sit down they'll be the one sitting at the far end of the table from you.

How you see yourself may not be how others see you

WARNING: *There are three types of people that you should make every effort, short of ending your own life, not to sit next to: anyone who as they speak spatters your face with half-chewed egg; anyone who has recently started divorce proceedings against you; anyone who is wearing a dress sword for the first time.*

A serviette can be useful when sitting next to someone with bad breath

Don't mention it

The Golden Rule in conversation is to avoid politics. If someone starts a political discussion there is only one remedy and that is to agree so strenuously on every point that it, like the Social Democrats, simply peters out for lack of interest. Or you can mention sex.

Sex trumps all other subjects and generally requires an evening of warm-up conversation before it is introduced. If advanced sexual positions are already being discussed over the soup don't be surprised if you find yourself hard up for conversation by the time the cheese arrives. That or in bed with seven relative strangers.

CHOOSE YOUR TOPIC CAREFULLY

WHO ARE THE WACKOS

BEHIND ALL THOSE

SCREWBALL COURT

DECISIONS?

WARNING: *If the conversation turns to sexual fantasies, under no circumstances reveal your own. If you do, you will be the object of continual derision well into the next century and you will be sent flippers in the post by anonymous jokers for years thereafter.*

The tricky thing about eating octopus is knowing where to start

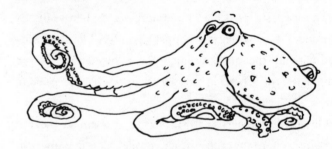

With dinner parties it's best to eat before you go. Everyone has something they simply can't eat and this invariably is what will be served. Say '*Oh God, I hate this*' if you've grown tired of social climbing and you've decided to try a bit of social free-fall. Otherwise try telling a joke so funny that no-one notices when you force your food down the waste disposal unit.

Spilling the beans

G ood hosts are braced for at least three spillages and it would be rude to disappoint them. The spill itself doesn't matter as good hosts will have arranged appropriate insurance. Concentrate on getting your reaction right. When you've walloped a glass of Bordeaux over the cream silk dress of your hostess, simply continue with your amusing anecdote, walk round behind her, unzip her dress, pull it smartly over her head and stuff it into the washing machine on a hot cycle.

Return to the table, refill your glass and subtly string out your anecdote to give you time for spin drying, ironing and any invisible mending. Work up to a big climax with plenty of French style gesticulating including one movement that involves pulling a dress over your hosts head.

DON'T PLAY WITH YOUR FOOD

ESSENTIAL SURVIVAL CHECKLIST:

1　Do you have Rubberised pockets for slipping stewed apricots into?

2　Will the other guests include anyone likely to make an attempt on your life?

3　Were a chicken bone to lodge fatally in your throat do you have immortal last words prepared that take into account difficulties in pronunciation attendant on having a drumstick wedged sideways in your oesophagus?

4　Do you pass wind to the left or right?

FIVE THINGS THAT IT IS MORE POLITE NOT TO EAT AT DINNER PARTIES:

1　Packed Lunches

2　Snot

3　Flower arrangements

4　Soft furnishings

5　Pets

Getting the hell out

Don't leave before you arrive. This sort of behaviour doesn't impress anybody. Leaving the table at any time before the end of the meal is generally frowned upon unless you've started having contractions. The offer of coffee is the polite way of saying, *'please be gone within half an hour.'* Once you've had your coffee, start making ritual leaving-type noises.

To be understood properly these must start with the word *'well'*. *'Well it's been a lovely evening,'* or *'Well it's getting late'*. Don't however follow *'well'* with something that will provoke further conversation: *'Well, it looks like the Pacific rim is emerging as a major trading bloc.'* If you get the *'well'* line right it will be followed by *'Are you sure you won't have another coffee?'* There is no more coffee. Stand up and start your goodbyes.

Don't start any goodbye kisses until you're standing at the front door. If you start kissing while you're still with the other guests you'll end up spending half an hour kissing everyone you've met, doing brief resumes of the embarrassing little conversations you had with them and coming out with appalling lies like promising to call them.

WARNING: *When you're finally outside you may well want to say 'Quite frankly I would have had more fun at home, staring at the cat litter.' Don't. Many hosts open a window at this point and can hear every word.*

Three weeks after the dinner party you'll discover whether or not you were a hit. If the next invitation comes from the charming sophisticated person you were oiling up to all night then you were. If it comes from the social leper who spent all night oiling up to you then you weren't.

Some goodbye kisses can be too late

2

DRIVING

- Breathtaking performance

- Original documents

- Excellent safety record

- Environmentally friendly

- Many security features

T rying to impress socially without a car is like high diving without a pool; however fancy your moves are, you still end up hurting yourself rather badly. It's difficult to be socially dazzling when you're in a bus queue wedged between old ladies carrying bags full of loose potatoes. Once you have a car, impressing people is a pretty simple business. The things to go for are speed, power and witty stickers.

IDEALLY GO FOR ALL THREE:

Have a Porsche with a sticker saying 'My other car's a Bentley'.

Breathtaking performance

In social circles the power of your car is roughly equivalent to your performance in bed. Driving an Austin Allegro is therefore a virtual admission of impotence. Basically you want a car so fast you can hardly get into it. But beware of bright red Italian sports cars that are incredibly low slung. If you drive over anything more prominent than a road marking you risk instant emasculation (unless you happen to be a woman). These cars can also be temperamental. This is Italian temperamental not British temperamental, i.e. turn the ignition and the car blows up.

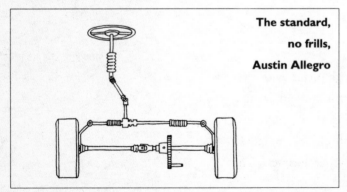

The standard, no frills, Austin Allegro

If you do have an incredibly fast car, don't forget the sticker for additional social leverage: *'If you can read this,*

I'm still in first.' Convertibles are only fun if you want to finish a drive looking like Ken Dodd.

Unless you like to spend a lot of time on hard shoulders, don't buy a second-hand car. Salesmen can be very persuasive and you can walk into a garage with £3000 and come out half an hour later with a cube of crushed metal that only moves with the aid of a powerful electro-magnet. Don't fall for the *'one lady driver'* scam. The driver they're referring to is Boadicea.

A good 2nd car if your first is an Austin Allegro

REMEMBER: *Never pay the asking price. Pick a fault and then haggle, preferably downwards. For example, 'I've noticed this car doesn't have an engine. Perhaps we could knock off a fiver.' Generally, watch out for car dealerships that incorporate the word 'scrap' in their trading name.*

Original documents

The Highway Code is like the Joy of Sex; everyone's read it but no one wants to be tested on it. This is a bit of a shame, because if you re-read it you'll find it's packed with fascinating information. For instance, flashing red lights at a level crossing mean that Supersaver tickets are not valid on that train. A broken white line with flashing orange lights on either side means that you are driving up the main runway at Heathrow. On the back cover there is a fascinating chart of stopping distances.

FOR EXAMPLE: *If you're travelling at seventy miles per hour in wet conditions and you drive into a huge concrete block your stopping distance is approximately four millimetres.*

The average car today is pretty well equipped, so if you are hoping to make an impression through your optional extras they have to be pretty exceptional. Something along the lines of a heated scrotum rest should do it. If you are in business, the way to impress is to simulate office conditions in your car. Faxes and phones in the car are pretty passé and you should really be looking to have a receptionist, an executive gym and an attractive plant-filled atrium.

The ultimate in-car entertainment is a head up display that projects your favourite video on to the windscreen as you drive. Every sixty seconds or so the screen goes blank to give you a chance to catch up with the latest position *vis-à-vis* other cars, pedestrians, crash barriers, and so forth.

FIVE SEXUAL POSITIONS

POSSIBLE IN A MINI:

1 Woman on top	3 Man in front seat, woman in back seat	5 Man in boot, woman in glove compartment
2 Man underneath	4 Woman in back seat, man in boot	

Excellent safety record

The work of statisticians has meant that the occasional accident is now inevitable. Don't feel bad if you knock a pedestrian over a hedge. In fact, make the most of it; sue them for leaving the scene of the crime. Also watch out for children on the road. They drive a lot faster than the rest of us. A simple point of driving etiquette is when you fall asleep at the wheel, try not to *snore*. This can be incredibly irritating to your passengers during the last few seconds of their lives.

Recently there have been a rash of safety innovations. These include steering wheels that collapse in a collision so that you won't hurt yourself. British Leyland got there first with the Austin Allegro, which was specially designed so that if it came into contact with anything firmer than a blancmange, it collapsed completely.

Italians are rightly proud of their reputation as the worst drivers in the world. Now that we are all moving ever closer to a single European state we can look forward to a lot more Italians on our roads and therefore we should know what to expect. Italian drivers regard having all four wheels on the road at the same time as being the height of Anglo-Saxon frigidity. It is a point of honour that the shortest drive down to the shops should include reversing at speed through a pedestrian precinct, losing both wing mirrors while accelerating between a police van and an oncoming lorry, and rolling the car sideways down a long flight of steps through a party of nuns.

Parking at the end of a car journey is looked upon by Italians as being similar to the last act of an opera; not complete without a lot of high pitched screeching and multiple deaths.

DON'T FORGET: *The average Italian believes that more progress is to be made through use of the horn than the gearbox.*

ALWAYS SIGNAL

I intend to deliver the Pizza to No. 8

I intend to deliver the Pizza to No. 9

Environmentally friendly

*A*ll cars now claim to be green. *The Mercedes 500 hits hedgehogs so fast that they die with less pain and it flattens them so completely that there's less waste.* Of course the Austin Allegro was the first environmentally friendly car. People who bought one generally travelled by foot or public transport.

A lot of research has gone into alternative ways of powering cars.

The first car powered by a controlled nuclear reaction is soon to be developed and the AA have already agreed to provide a service by which if you have a meltdown on the motorway they will cover your car in 16ft of concrete and seal off one hundred square miles of the surrounding countryside for the next five hundred years. In the meantime the Japanese have invented a car that works by plugging it into its own cigar lighter.

WARNING: *All manufacturers publish ridiculously unrealistic fuel consumption figures which are based on cars driven daintily on polished surfaces by nuns in aerodynamic wimples.*

THE FIVE MOST COMMON DRIVING MISTAKES:

1 Deciding to take a short cut round the M25

2 Putting a sticker in the window saying: *'I like traffic wardens. PS. Back in five minutes'*

3 Confusing the colour green and red

4 Flicking a V sign at a truck driver when you're both in a traffic jam

5 Attempting to overtake in an Austin Allegro

Crossing at a Pelican Crossing

DON'T WALK

WALK

RUN

INFORM NEXT OF KIN

Many security features

H aving your car stolen is good news for three reasons: *firstly, it means you had a car worth stealing; secondly, you can dream up the mother of all insurance claims; and lastly, it gives the rest of us an extra parking space.* These days you are judged on the quality of your anti-theft device. A good one is the engine immobiliser (a permanent feature on the Allegro). The latest one is a little box called the *'Heavy Breather'* that steams up the windows and rocks the car rhythmically, giving the impression that it is occupied.

WARNING: *The drawback with this device is that it can begin to lose its credibility after twelve hours of continuous use.*

Many radios now have an anti-theft device that senses when the radio is being tampered with and locks it onto Melody FM thus rendering it useless.

Philosophers say that it is better to travel than to arrive. This is probably because philosophers never get invited to good parties. (And let's face it, someone who doubts their own existence is hardly likely to be the life and soul of the party.) Social climbers know that arriving in the right car at the right place in the right manner is everything. That's why when the Queen rolls up to a charity première she doesn't mount the kerb, stall the car, bang her head on the sill, slam her dress in the door and then wander off leaving her Allegro belching smoke over the cheering masses.

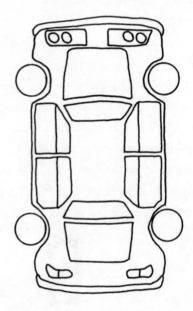

The Allegro suspension was not designed with vigorous sexual activity in mind

3

COUNTRY WEEKENDS

- What is the Country?

- What should one wear?

- What should one drive?

- What does one do?

- How should one leave?

A n essential step on the social ladder is a country weekend with the landed classes. Unfortunately, country weekends are modelled on life on the Somme: the key elements are cold, mud and senseless waste of human life.

What is the country?

The country is divided into two halves. One half is owned by people who spend other people's money and do nothing with the land; these are farmers. The other half is owned by the landed classes. You can tell which sort of country you're in by a quick check on the animals: Horses, dogs and pheasants, you're OK; cows, pigs and men with sideburns, move on smartly.

Some parts of the country don't qualify as *'the country'*. For example it's fine to say you're spending the weekend in Scotland but not in Wales. This is probably because there's nothing to shoot in Wales. Apart from the Welsh, that is, and that went out of fashion in the thirteenth century.

WARNING: *Not all English counties qualify as the country either. You won't impress anyone by saying you're having a country weekend in Essex.*

How does one get there? Drive along a motorway for about a hundred miles and then turn off on to a smaller road. Keep turning off on to ever smaller roads until you run over a chicken. You're there.

Once you're in the country, getting round is impossible. During the war they rearranged the country to confuse possible invaders but they forgot to put it back. Asking a local won't help as they've got centuries of inbreeding to cope with. The best you can expect is: *'Red sky at night, your duvet's alight'*.

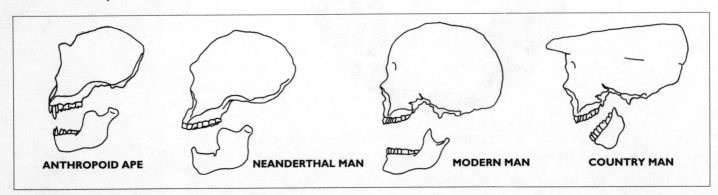

ANTHROPOID APE   **NEANDERTHAL MAN**   **MODERN MAN**   **COUNTRY MAN**

What should one wear?

The country dress code stipulates that all clothes must be green, must irritate the skin, and must have more natural oils than Kuwait. Not only must they not look new, they must look as though they've never been new. To get this effect drop the garment on the cow shed floor and then drive over it a couple of times in your Range Rover.

There's no point going to the country without a waxed jacket. And to really impress you must know the exact function of all those surplus belts, flaps and pockets. Real country people undo that little stud under the left armpit before engaging a Land Rover's four-wheeled drive.

Where does one sleep? If you've studied the art of sleeping in the freezer you'll be fine. *'We've put you in the blue room,'* means that when you wake up, your flesh will be that colour.

WARNING: *(A couple of extra blankets won't help.) In the country extra blankets work on the Wall's Viennetta principle: The more layers, the colder it is.*

One of the interesting side effects of the cold is that it shrinks your bladder to the size of a Smartie. When you go to the loo at three in the morning you will discover that every floorboard lets the rest of the house know exactly where you're going, that however low you stoop there's a beam slightly lower, and that flushing the loo activates the loudest clanking in plumbing history. A fourth thing you only discover in the morning. The loo that you thought was just at the end of the corridor was in fact en suite in your hosts' bedroom. When you stood there for five minutes with your pyjama bottoms round your ankles aiming vaguely downwards, your hosts were quietly sitting up in bed praying that you had exceptional night vision.

'Just come down to breakfast when you're ready.' This is country shorthand for see you at dawn. And when you do stagger downstairs with your underpants on back to front, don't expect cornflakes, or toast or anything edible Country people make it a point of honour to have strange things for breakfast like kipper and kidneys. This is a good time to get friendly with the dogs. On the subject of animals, country people think that all animals are essentially recalcitrant pets, and will happily stand by as a badger eats your car tyres.

What should one drive?

W hatever you drive in the country is fine, as long as it's a Land Rover or a Range Rover. The only people that drive normal cars are farmers, and what do they know about the country. Cars work on the same principles as waxed jackets. Unless they look as if they've been in the family since the relief of Mafeking they're simply not on. This is especially the case with Land Rovers. Your status in the country is proportional to the number of bits you have missing from your Land Rover. You'll get all sorts of brownie points if you've been driving around for months without a steering wheel. Of course, this has to be accompanied by the appropriate loving remark; *'Do you know she dropped her big end in a field last autumn, and you would hardly notice.'* Land Rovers are like everyone's favourite old dog; no one's prepared to be the first to say *'She smells and she needs to be put down.'* Another thing that country people never, ever say is *'I'm going to wash the car this morning.'*

In conversation the mention of anything about the city or normal life as lived by 99% of the population is exceptionally bad form. As far as possible stick to weather, dogs and the effect of weather on dogs.

Country people think its incredibly funny to have names that no one in their right mind can pronounce. Before you go to the country you should know that *'The Rt.Hon. Ralph Cholmondeley-Bottomley'* is pronounced Rafe Chumly-Bumly. Or Pedigree Chum to his mates.

10 THINGS YOU'RE NOT REALLY ALLOWED TO SHOOT IN THE COUNTRY BUT IT'S DAMNED GOOD FUN IF YOU DO:		
1 Farmers	5 New Age Travellers	9 Country vicars
2 Farmers' wives	6 Cows	10 Anyone in bright coloured
3 Yokels	7 Ecologists	clothing
4 Ramblers	8 Outward bound schools	

What does one do?

H orse riding is enormously popular in the country. It's based on the premise that the horse trots, gallops and jumps things for no apparent reason and you sit on its back like a lemon.

WARNING: *Make sure you know the vital commands. To go: Yaah! Hyup! Gadip! Oh for Pete's sake get on with it! To stop: Whoa! Whoa there! Whoa betide you if you don't stop right now!* If you find horse riding insufficiently dull, try fishing.

Don't however, make the mistake of thinking that the sort of fishing country people do is in any way related to the fishing that millions of ordinary people do. Country people fish for salmon even when they're standing five feet from a sewage outlet. If they accidentally catch a working class fish, such as a haddock or a cod, they throw it back immediately.

It's also a point of honour among country people not to sit on the bank. They have to stand in the river, which is like shooting grouse whilst standing in their nest. Therefore, the taller your waders are the better. Top country fishers have waders laced up to their throat and fish with only their heads visible. Vigorous casting often leads to drowning.

Shooting things is another important part of country life. But country people are very specific about pheasants. If you see one of these beautiful birds in the hedgerow you must let it go peacefully about its business. But if it takes off you can shoot the bastard. Pheasants know this and when the shooting season gets under way they stop flying altogether and, whenever possible, take public transport.

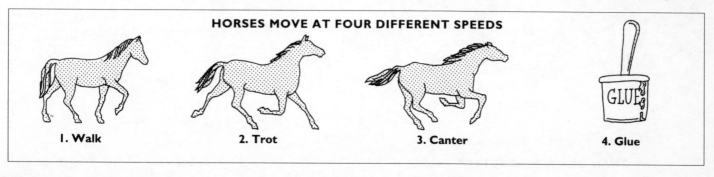

HORSES MOVE AT FOUR DIFFERENT SPEEDS

1. Walk   2. Trot   3. Canter   4. Glue

How should one leave?

T heoretically sex should be a popular country pastime. In fact, country weekends are a form of contraception. Country people wear so many layers that undressing them is no more erotic than pass-the parcel.

WARNING: *Coupling with country people can be a disappointment, because after a life time of punishment in the saddle, their reproductive equipment has all the sensitivity of a frying pan.*

By Sunday evening your metabolic rate will be so low that, had you been in the office, you would be assumed to be dead. This is no excuse for forgetting the most important part of the weekend. As you drive out, there will be a large pool of slurry in your way. City dwellers instinctively avoid it. Country people drive straight through to cover their car in glitch so that they won't be mistaken for city dwellers when they park in the office car park on Monday.

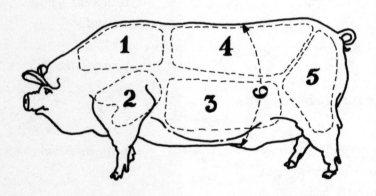

**A PIG HAS MORE EROGENOUS ZONES
THAN ONE WOULD EXPECT**

FIVE SOURCES OF POISON IN THE COUNTRY
1 Deadly nightshade
2 Canadian Moonseed
3 Jewelweed
4 Monks-hood
5 Mrs. Verity Cussons, The Rose Cottage, Hambleden

4

FAMILY

- *Our father who art in the shed*

- *Bundles of sticky joy*

- *Suffer little children*

- *Bad skin – bad attitude*

- *Grandparents*

- *School*

- *Leaving home*

T raditionally children were born into a two parent family, which was like a one-parent family, only twice as bad. Nowadays, family members can be divided into three types; those who have had children, those who are children, and those that sit in a brown armchair behind the living room door smelling slightly suspect.

Our father who art in the shed

E very family needs a stern father figure to provide discipline, make the decisions and generally run the whole family. This role is generally undertaken by the mother. Fortunately there is another role, which involves allotments, pubs and fishing rods and fathers often find themselves drawn to this.

When children are growing up, it is enormously important that they have good communication with their father, which is why fathers should always leave a forwarding address. Fathers are good for passing on the important lessons that help you through life, like how to corner safely with a heavily laden wheelbarrow. Mothers are great for emotional support. If you ever argue with a boyfriend or girlfriend your mum will always be there; in fact that's generally what the arguments are about.

WARNING: *The downside of all this caring can be that sometimes mothers can be overprotective. If you're approaching sixteen and she is still X-raying eggs to check for dangerous hard bits, start to worry.*

When you are young, you ask all sorts of extremely difficult questions such as: '*Mum, do you think the origin of the universe will ever be discovered?*' But however difficult the questions are, mothers will always have the answer: '*It won't be if you don't clean your room.*'

You can always rely on your family for a frank and honest opinion

Bundles of sticky joy

T he reason why men like to sleep immediately after ejaculation is that they know they're going to get precious little of it nine months later. When babies first arrive home they sleep for eighteen hours a day, waking only to emit thick, green bile from the orifice of their choice. Many couples have more than one baby to check whether they all do this. They do.

When you are a baby you are fed a thick paste from a special mixer. It's only years later that you discover that this special mixer was the waste disposal unit. Babies have a very powerful effect on women. However sophisticated, worldly and powerful women are in their working lives, when they go and visit their friends' babies, they cluck.

**Plumbers have a special spanner
to bleed your current account**

8 NAMES NO ONE UNDER 50 HAS:	8 NAMES NO ONE OVER 50 HAS:
Reginald	Wayne
Horace	Darren
Alf	Kevin
Mildred	Cool-J
Dot	Demi
Sylvester	Farrah
Faith	Ronella
Caligula	Sonic

Suffer little children

One of the great unsolved mysteries of childhood is how to reconcile the two statements '*Go and play outside*' with '*Why have you trodden mud through the house?*'

When you're a child you get inundated with lots of good advice like, '*Never speak to strangers or accept sweets from them*'. This makes the first day at school incredibly difficult. Children develop fierce dislikes to certain foods, generally anything that contains proteins or vitamins. The only way to get them to eat green stuff is to insist that they must have a clean plate. The upshot of this is that parents spend the next ten years removing Brussels sprouts from the bottom of vases and little blocks of frozen prunes from the freezer.

Now that flogging is out of fashion, a good way of disciplining your children is with the colourful magnetic letters you put on your fridge. Spell out your will on the fridge and, if they don't behave themselves, change it so that the neighbours get the stereo.

WARNING: *A word of advice to parents about punishing your children: if it hurts you more than it hurts them, then you're doing it wrong.*

For some reason no one has ever quite fathomed, children like to collect small furry animals as pets. Be especially careful with hamsters, rabbits and guinea pigs, especially when you get two of them together for mating purposes. If after a few months nothing has happened, pick one up, turn it over and have a closer look. What you thought was a female guinea pig may in fact be a male leopard.

REMEMBER: *Goldfish do not make good pets as they die when in contact with water.*

PETS stuck on outer branches should not be humoured

Bad skin – bad attitude

A teenager can have no greater curse than trendy parents. *'I want to be your friend, just call me Sarah,'* is the last thing a teenager wants to hear from his father. If you have hippies as parents the only form of rebellion you have available is deliberately and provocatively reading the Financial Times in front of them, and constantly asking them about the merits or otherwise of ERM membership.

On the other hand, traditional disciplinarian parents create their own problems.

Teenagers who are constantly told not to answer back, in later life often have great difficulty using the telephone. It's most embarrassing when your parents take you aside and try to explain all about sex and contraception, especially when you're living, breathing proof that they don't know the first thing about it.

WARNING: *Expect your first lecture on contraception shortly after you have presented your parents with their first grandchild.*

Grandparents are like grand pianos. They're obviously very nice but you wouldn't want to have one permanently in your front room. The incredible thing about grandparents is how old they are. You can be having a perfectly normal conversation about something and they will chime in with *'I remember the coronation of Henry the Second.'* One of the compensations of having children is that it allows you to call your parents *'Grandpa'* and *'Grandma'*.

Many family holidays get no further than the cross-channel ferry

Grandparents

A mongst the tragedies of old age is the gradual deterioration in critical faculties. You can send your grandfather out for a newspaper and he will come back with the Daily Express. Grandparents often get afflicted with a disease that makes movement very difficult for long stretches of the day. It's called Bingo.

One thing grandparents are excellent at is evoking our imperial past at the drop of a hat, which is one reason why no one wears hats anymore. There are, on the other hand, some things grandparents never say; For example: *'Wow, that's cheap.'* Remember too, that once everyone's grandparents have died, no one will know what dripping is

Every family, however happy, is cursed with an Uncle Mike. Uncle Mike never married because he is a walking public health nuisance. According to Uncle Mike though, he never married because he has shrapnel lodged in his groin. It's one of his inexhaustible fund of war stories that tend to lose credibility in the light of the public knowledge that his services were dispensed with by the military *'in the interests of general morale'*. Uncle Mike stays with the family at Christmas because no one has ever discovered a deterrent sufficiently powerful to keep him away. Uncle Mike's best friends are all from the council's pest control department, which run a training centre in his kitchen.

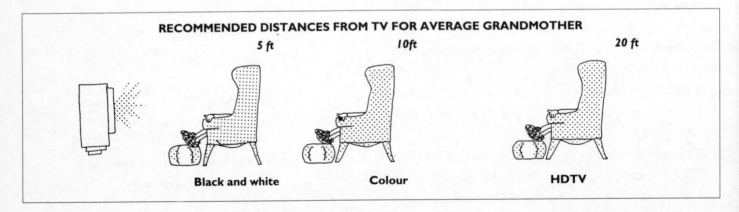

RECOMMENDED DISTANCES FROM TV FOR AVERAGE GRANDMOTHER

5 ft   10 ft   20 ft

Black and white   **Colour**   **HDTV**

School

S| chool can be the best days of your life, if you happen to die young. Schools are inevitably a big part of family life, and the school report can be a source of friction, especially if your teacher writes things such as, *'Evans would do a lot better if he hadn't come from the same shallow gene pool as his parents.'*

Secondary schools are holding camps to keep young people off the street while their hormones kick in. Choosing schools in the first place is very important. Look out for schools where the prospectus is written by the Serious Crime Squad and the school uniform is a body bag. Being successful at primary school gives you a great head start in life. For some people, being milk monitor will be the high point of their life and they will never shake off the milk monitor mentality. Collectively these people are known as MPs.

As a child, one often has to take a day off for very important reasons like the need to hang around with one's mates. The following day, when you get dragged up in front of the headmaster, it's worth remembering that a watertight excuse is: *'I wasn't playing truant, I was contracting out.'*

One of the low points of school life is exchange trips. This is where they try to match you up with someone a bit like you only foreign, and you end up spending a week in a French young offenders institution.

5 BENEFITS NOT GENERALLY ASSOCIATED WITH BEING A MEMBER OF A FAMILY BUT WORTH REMEMBERING ANYWAY:
1 In a family of four, you only have to take out the dustbin once a month
2 There is always someone on hand to blame when you've accidentally burnt the house down
3 You've got a better chance of being in somebody's will
4 If you're all involved in a nasty car crash there's a greater likelihood that at least one member of the family will see the funny side
5 It gives the rest of life a rosier hue

Leaving home

L eaving home can be a terribly traumatic time. For the first time you have to make mature and responsible decisions about where to live, how to earn a living and how to develop a network of supporting contacts. This can all be very intimidating when you've just turned six.

When you do finally leave home at eighteen, your parents will give you incredibly tactless presents such as recipe books called *'One is Fun'* packed with jolly little recipes such as *'Take an egg. Break it. Shoot yourself.'*

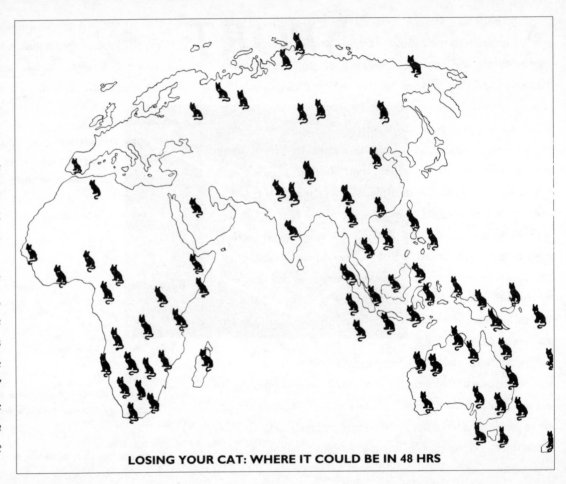

LOSING YOUR CAT: WHERE IT COULD BE IN 48 HRS

5

SPORT

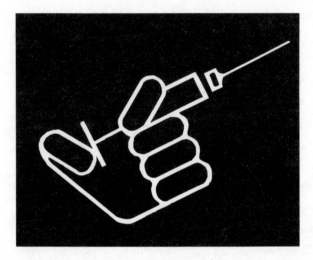

- *Kicking the habit*

- *Straight bat to the pavilion*

- *Running sore*

- *So called sports*

- *Fit fat*

S ports can be divided into those that are designed to hurt, degrade and embarrass your opponent, and those that are designed to injure, debase and humiliate your opponent. When competing in sport always bear in mind that it's not the winning that's important, it's the taking part; which was the motto they had on the wall during the Nuremberg war trials.

Kicking the habit

Martial arts are all about drawing together the forces of nature into a mystical balance within yourself and then kicking someone in the groin. Something you should never ask a black belt is *'If you're so tough why are you wearing your pyjamas?'*. There are lots of eastern martial arts, and every so often a new one comes along such as Thai kick boxing, where you use both your feet and your fists to fight. It's still a bit of a mystery why Glasgow Scrapping has never caught on in the east as it requires the use of fists, feet, head, teeth, bottles, iron bars, etc. Perhaps it's because our eastern friends have never seen the logic of the head butt. After all the head is usually protected in a fight and therefore the head butt has the same logic as trying to derail a train with your testicles.

Olympic swimmers don't actually swim much faster than the rest of us. What they have done is master three things: diving in wearing goggles without losing an eyeball; tumble turning at the end of the pool without jamming a foot in one of the water inlets; and breathing to the side without swallowing half a litre of water and having to hang on to the ropes coughing like a dervish. British swimmers never do particularly well because we

don't have that many swimming pools. But if there was a race which demanded swimming through frog spawn, round half submerged shopping trolleys while trying to pull fishing hooks out of your trunks, we would get a chestful of medals.

BOXING:
Haymakers
will rarely
take your
opponent
by surprise

Straight bat to the pavilion

F or the English, cricket is an annual extended punishment for ever having an Empire. A cricket match is divided into two halves. The first half is when the touring side go into bat and amass a total of approximately 600 for the loss of one or two wickets, depending on how bored the batsmen get. After a break for tea, England go into bat, are bowled out for 16 and everyone has a second cup of tea. Some people think cricket is enormously complex and that it's frightfully amusing to explain it to Americans. These people should remember that if Americans were capable of understanding cricket they would be playing it, rather than showing a curious preference for rounders in tights.

Rugby is increasingly popular as a spectator sport. After a good game many spectators run on to the pitch and collect teeth and bones and bits of flesh. After a couple of seasons, serious collectors can put together a complete rugby player.

Rugby is a notoriously tough game. In a famous game before the war, a fly half did a tackle so fierce that it killed every man in both teams. Naturally the fly half was sent off with the result that the game lost some of its sparkle.

Because it's a macho game any form of emotion is frowned on.

FOR EXAMPLE: *If you score a match winning try in an international there would be none of the protracted snogging and petting you get amongst football players. In rugby you're allowed to celebrate by smiling grimly at the nurse in the intensive care unit.*

After the match the smallest member of the team is elected to take all the kit to be washed at the local blood transfusion centre.

EIGHT SPORTS AND THE CALORIES THEY CONSUME IN ONE MINUTE		
1	Rowing (eights)	3214
2	Rowing (marital)	1657
3	Clay pigeon shooting (man)	119
4	Clay pigeon shooting (pigeon)	3245
5	Golfing	23
6	Caddying	2897
7	Darts	2
8	Eating chocolate profiteroles	−5746

Running sore

R unning is very relaxing until you see another runner coming in the opposite direction. Inevitably you both speed up to show how super fit you are and find yourselves with a closing speed of approaching fifty miles per hour. When you've passed each other, you both veer off into the nearest bush and cough blood for half an hour. Marathon running is one of the most gruelling sports known to man, although women don't have too much difficulty.

Most average runners hit the wall at about twenty miles. Why they haven't changed the route to avoid it is a very good question. For those that find marathons a little too easy, there is the triathlon where you cycle fifty miles, swim two miles and then run a marathon. If this weren't enough there is an even more gruelling sport called the quadrathlon where you cycle fifty miles, swim two miles, run a marathon and then have a game of badminton.

TENNIS 1: SUCCESSFUL SEASONS START WITH STRINGING RACKETS

FOUR INJURIES YOU ARE UNLIKELY TO SUSTAIN IN PING PONG NO MATTER HOW VIGOROUSLY YOU PLAY IT:

1   Fractured skull
2   Crushed rib cage
3   Massive internal haemorrhaging
4   Broken back and shattered vertebrae

So-called sports

S ynchronised swimming is an enormously popular sport but not quite as popular as the sport of holding synchronised swimmers underwater to see how long it takes before they stop smiling. Bungee jumping is another growth sport. This was first inadvertently discovered by Brian Bungee whose attempt to commit suicide by hurling himself from Sydney Harbour bridge was thwarted by the elastic in his underpants snagging on the balustrade.

SWIMMING:
A critical
underwater
hazard is
forgetting
your trunks

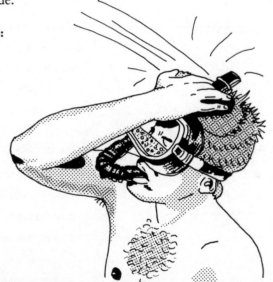

Modesty in
beach wear
can be overdone

Croquet is a horrifying game and is currently under investigation by the League Against Cruel Sports. It's no coincidence that four out of the last five croquet world champions went on to be policy advisers to Pol Pot. The fifth, by the way, was killed in a horrific off the ball incident. A new sport that has taken off in recent years is one in which you go off to a remote part of the country, dress up in combat gear, divide into two teams and use pretend guns to capture a flag. This is called the Territorial Army.

Fit fat

F itness and sport part company at the pub door. Of the body's three thousand different muscle groups, throwing a dart requires two. Extraordinarily, they are exactly the same two required for picking your nose and flicking a V sign. Playing darts looks deceptively easy. But as a beginner, the first dart you throw is likely to execute some fancy aerobatics before nose-diving into the pint of the vicious humourless thug out on probation. Snooker is basically the same as hockey in that you use a special stick to whack the ball into the back of the net. With snooker you have the additional handicap of a bloody great table in the way.

TENNIS 2: GETTING IN THE
RIGHT POSITION

Fruit machines work on the same principle as electricity meters. You feed in your coins and you get fancy lights saying 'Win! Win! Win!'. After a while the money runs out, and if you want more lights saying 'Win! Win! Win!' you have to feed the meter. In many pubs there are trivia games where you put your money in and the machine asks you what your selection is. If you say Don MacLean you are wrong and have to sit down.

A sport wildly popular amongst young teenagers is snogging. For this you have two teams, one of which is a boy and the other a girl. The game takes place on the sofa and starts when the mouths are pressed together. The object of the game is then to steer the other person off the sofa, across the carpet and round the rest of the furniture simply by the power of your snog.

RULES: *Tongues are permissible for added leverage but dribbling is a bookable offence. If for some reason one team touches the other team's breast, this is handball and the game has to restart. The game is over when one of the teams knocks over a standard lamp and wakes up the baby they are supposed to be sitting. In certain Middle East countries this game carries the death penalty.*

6

AIR TRAVEL

- Flying Waiters
- Women and children
- Watch where you sit
- First Love
- Down and out

Modern passenger planes are little class systems hurtling around at 30,000ft. Flights in them inspire feats of social climbing that, were they to be recorded in the black box, would shock the toughest crash investigator.

Flying waiters

C heck-in times three hours before departure are for people who enjoy airport breakfasts. They have been devised to increase sales in the Duty Free Shop and should, like visa requirements, be studiously ignored. Real travellers get up shortly after the final call, arrange any necessary innoculations, and then make their way to the airport. It's worth remembering that planes don't actually take off until three or four minutes after departure time. Taxiing for take-off means that, just like taxis, you can hail them and jump on board.

DON'T FORGET: *When you check in, stride up to the desk and insist on a particular seat, like 14G. It helps to know where this seat is, or you can find yourself stuffed in a canvas jump seat flying backwards to New Zealand.*

Don't worry about what sort of suitcases you have as experienced travellers don't bother with them at all. Just pretend you haven't had time to pack and empty your laundry basket on the check-in desk. You can also create an impression by checking-in obscure items like standard lamps and lawnmowers. If they refuse to take them, or refuse to comply with any other unreasonable request, always respond with, '*Well, you'll have to bump me up to First.*'

If you insist on suitcases, always make sure that your hand luggage is four times the size of your other cases. It should also be heavy enough to kill or maim when it plummets from the overhead locker during the safety announcement.

WARNING: *If you're taking anything delicate, it's best to smash it up before you pack, as baggage handlers exhibit the sort of co-ordination unlikely to impress the England Test selectors.*

Heathrow Terminal 5 will be financed by the private sector

Women and children

M ost flights now have something called pre-boarding, when the first people allowed on are the elderly, people with special needs, and families with young children. The fact that you specified added Tabasco with your meal at check-in does not qualify you as having special needs. However, what you can do is take advantage of the increasing number of one-parent families travelling these days. When you see one of these making their way to the gate, fall in behind them, give the smallest one a clip round the ear and say *'That's enough of that, Jonathan'*. Alternatively you can come to the airport with your luggage stuffed into a papoose, with your tennis shorts cleverly arranged to look like a baby's bonnet. If you're trying this method, remember not to fling your papoose into the X-ray machine.

On any flight the key thing is to prove how bored you are by the whole thing. If the person next to you turns the lights off and pulls up his blanket, trump him by changing into your Captain Pugwash pyjamas and slinging a hammock from the overhead lockers so that your bottom regularly bumps against his forehead. If he's already asleep, turn all three air nozzles on him at full blast so that when you land in sunny Miami he's lost the end of his nose to frostbite.

REMEMBER: *The hallmark of the inexperienced traveller is this naive belief that there is enough room to squeeze past the drinks trolley when it's in the aisle.*

Many an airborne genital has met its Waterloo on the corner of these little steel monsters.

Beware of businessmen in Economy. They sell small shiny things without which we'd all be in the dark ages. If you feel they're winding up to ten hours of sales patter, make a big play of readying your barf-bag for action.

Soviet Airliners were designed around Aeroflot Stewardesses

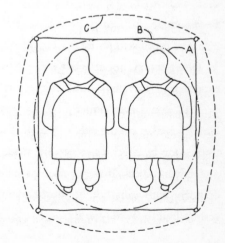

Watch where you sit

*I*n-flight movies are generally a repeat of the film you saw the night before the flight. If you haven't seen it, the person next to you will have and will be doing his sponsored getting up and down and pushing past you competition. If he samples bits of the film, laugh uproariously every time he takes his headphones off so that he has to whip them back on to see what he has missed. Never assume the seat in front of you is empty. Over Greenland a child's face will appear over the back, smile at you and then throw up into your lunch. When he has recovered he will play rocking chairs with his seat. If you tire of this, reach under his seat and inflate his life-jacket.

To relieve cramp during flights some airlines encourage people to do aerobics in their seat. The first thing you will know about this is when the seat in front of you shoots backwards and your complimentary red wine drains into your spanking new holiday trousers. If this happens take up your own form of exercise; pull on a pair of boxing gloves and beat the hell out of their headrest.

Going to the toilet is always a tricky business in the air, unless you're a pigeon. Just as your bladder reaches '*full*', you will hit heavy turbulence and you will be asked to stay in your seat and fasten your seatbelt. Four hours later, when the captain decides that perhaps there's not going to be any turbulence after all, you join the queue of approximately 120 people for the loo. You get to third in line when it is announced that you are about to land and would you please return to your seat and fasten your seat belt. It is about this time that a stewardess will lean over your seat, smile and say '*you shouldn't have had all those free drinks, should you.*'

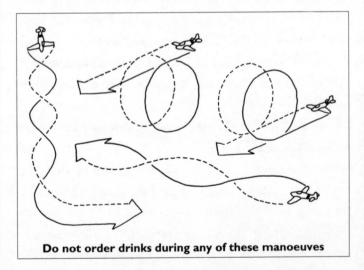

Do not order drinks during any of these manoeuves

First love

T hose who can't afford a seat in First or business class have their own special class called 'Cargo'. Having a seat here is not the end of the world as you've got the rest of the flight to get into First. It's no good trying to sneak in wedged in the drinks trolley or waiting until your halfway across the Atlantic and then walking into First class as if you've just boarded saying 'Sorry I'm late'. Instead, try gross over-reaction to the mildest turbulence by staggering up and down the length of the airplane as if you were in a wildly pitching ship. By the time you've crashed through the dividing curtains a couple of times, no one will remember whether you started in First or Economy. But be careful you don't overdo it and go lurching straight into the cockpit, especially when you're landing in fog.

Welsh independence could have grave consequences for Air Traffic Control standards

If you've actually paid for a First class ticket you can't have people thinking you're just another business person on a corporate freebie. Wear a loud Hawaiian shirt and sing, 'We're off to sunny, sunny Spain'. This is especially effective on flights to Moscow.

THE 5 MOST COMMON CAUSES OF AIR SICKNESS	
I	Airline food
2	An eleven hour flight next to a Jehovah's Witness
3	The boiled sweets they give you for your ears
4	Travel agents who tell you they're booked you on Air Guatemala
5	Stall turns in a 747

INTERNATIONALLY RECOGNISED SIGNS

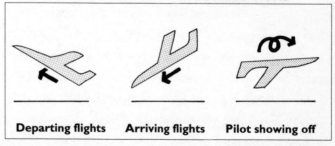

Departing flights   **Arriving flights**   **Pilot showing off**

Down and out

W hen you start to make your descent, some people have the nasty habit of relieving the pressure in their ears by holding their noses and blowing. If they start doing this, talk to them but without any noise. With a bit of luck they'll think they've gone deaf, grab their nose and blow the back of their head off.

Don't wait for the plane to get to the terminal to start getting your things together. Wait until the flight attendants are strapped in for landing and then stand up, get your luggage down and wait calmly by the main door. Train commuters can try the old trick of holding the door slightly open before the plane comes to a standstill.

At passport control there is often a large queue and it is almost inevitable that the person in front of you will be an evil smelling student, in-bound from Colombia who is sweating heavily and is about to give the airport sniffer-dogs the high of a life-time. Don't bother swapping queues, as you will only find yourself behind a large third world family each with seven huge suitcases who are going to try and get through on a clumsily forged seven day holiday visa. Once you do get to the desk, the officer will flick to your photo and then give you a cursory glance.

Years of experience suggest that this is not the moment to say, 'What the hell are you looking at, shorty?'

In Baggage Reclaim you don't have to watch every case coming through. The arrival of your luggage will be heralded by a pair of your underpants cruising nonchalantly round the carousel. If your case arrives intact remember that baggage handlers often add anvils to your luggage. This is so they can have a laugh when you try and pull it manfully off the carousel with one hand and there is a loud crack as your spine snaps. In the arrivals hall people hold up signs because they don't know who the hell they're looking for. Select a driver with a peaked cap and say, 'I'm Mr Wakimura. Let's go'.

5 GOOD REASONS WHY FIGHTER PILOTS DON'T MAKE GOOD AIRLINE PILOTS	
1	Tendency to shout 'Tally Ho!' shortly before landing
2	Extreme nervousness on flights to Iraq
3	Tendency to fly in close-knit formations with other 747s
4	Won't fly more than 10ft above the ground
5	Overwhelming desire to do victory rolls after successful flights

7

SHOPPING

Hello,
Buy Me

- Ye olde shoppe

- You're going to pay for this

- Not my department

- No lingering

- Off your trolley

W hat sets mankind apart from animals is our ability to shop. Our behaviour in January sales puts us somewhere below the dung beetle. Shopping is the crucial interface between how wealthy you are and how much taste you have and is therefore one of the key elements in social survival.

Ye olde shoppe

Quaint old shoppes are very popular places to visit, browse around, pick up things, put things back down, chat to the owner and leave empty handed. That's why there are so few of them left. When you enter these shops two things happen simultaneously: firstly, you bang your head on a sign that says *'Duck or Grouse'*, you decide you hate the shop and all like it everywhere, and vow never to shop in one like it ever again as long as you live; secondly, some blithering, dithering idiot in an oatmeal cardigan and half moon glasses emerges from the gloom and warns you to mind your head.

If his array of hand-tooled leather key fobs had ever been attractive to you, they won't be now. The general rule is that the fewer items in the shop window the more expensive it is.

WARNING: *Never shop anywhere that doesn't price their stock. This gives shop 'assistants' a chance to play their special game of 'ballpark figures' where they make up a price based on how loaded you appear. You won't get round this by trying to look poor. They will think up some monstrous price designed not only to get you out of the shop, but also to make you wonder if there's any point in going on with life.*

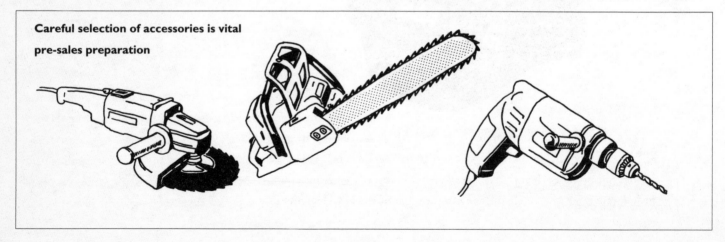

Careful selection of accessories is vital pre-sales preparation

You're going to pay for this

S ome shops make it their business to discourage custom. On entering one of these establishments you will be left to stew in your own inadequacy for a while and then someone infinitely superior to you in every way will condescend to ask whether they can help you, in a tone that implies that nothing can possibly help you.

**FOUR LINES SHOP ASSISTANTS
LOVE TO HEAR**

1 Do you accept milk tokens

2 I bought this miracle of modern engineering from you five minutes ago and it blew up in the car park, killing seven people

3 I'm in the film business. I've been watching you for the last ten minutes and I have to tell you that you have no future in films

4 I don't have much money but I'd like you to tell me about everything in the shop

---

They also leave the end of the question trailing, so that it sounds like the complete sentence would have been *'Can I help you back onto the street, sir?'* If you don't get things straight at this point, you never will. Ask breezily *'Are you a shop assistant?'* They may behave like ladies in waiting, but technically they're still shop assistants. If they respond haughtily that they're the manager, say *'Well done!!'* in a very enthusiastic way that implies that last week they were packing boxes.

The ridiculous thing about these exclusive shops is that they're very unwilling to take your money. Pull out a wodge of tenners and you're likely to be met with the response *'We don't accept cash, sir.'*

WARNING: *In these places, cash implies you are a pimp or a drug dealer.*

The done thing is to have an account, which implies that your great grandparents were pimps and drug dealers. These shops positively relish customers who don't pay, and they all have stories about one charming old gentleman who comes in here every week, orders a tweed suit, hasn't paid a penny since the war, and is one of our very best customers, oh yes.

Not my department

G oing into an expensive jewellers is a very good way to see whether you really want to get married. When you walk into the shop with that stunned, stupid look engaged couples have, the assistants all crowd round and whinny at you. One of their first questions will be about where you intend to get married and if your answer doesn't feature Westminster Abbey or St. Paul's, someone in the back will start dusting off the *'cheap'* tray. There are two vital lines in the wedding process. The easy one is in the park on one knee, and is a variation on *'Cynthia, will you marry me?'* The difficult one is in the jewellers on two knees, and is a variation on *'Have you anything cheaper.'* If you ask the second question, you can expect, *'Has sir tried Halfords?'*, and a very shaky start to married life.

The unbridgeable gulf between men and women is at its widest when it comes to clothes shopping. When men say they want to buy a pair of underpants, what women never understand is that what men really want is not the underpants themselves, but the whole experience of shopping for underpants; the joy of going from shop to shop comparing prices and styles, trying them on, seeing how they feel, perhaps considering a designer that they

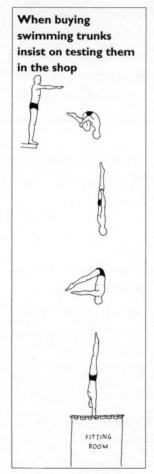

When buying swimming trunks insist on testing them in the shop

FITTING ROOM

know is a bit beyond their price range but wearing them anyway for a few minutes in front of the mirror, so they can remember how they would look in them if only they had the money; then perhaps having a leisurely cup of coffee and a croissant, and flicking through the brochures to discuss what's available, what's new, what's in, and what's out. And if at the end of the day we don't manage to buy any underpants at all, then that's fine, because its the looking that's important. When women understand that this is how men think, then shopping together will be more of a pleasure and less of a chore, and men won't be rushed into buying plain white Y-fronts all the time.

No lingering

*I*f you're wondering why Woolworth's has disappeared round the U-bend of the department store world, look no further than their perfume counter. Where is it? Who knows. All you can see from the street are boys' school trousers and liquorice allsorts at 10p a quarter. Unless you're a schoolboy with 10p you are most unlikely to go in.

Most other department stores realise that putting the perfume counters next to the front doors lends the whole shop an ambience of quality and luxury. They also make it impossible to leave, as every turn is blocked by heavily made up ladies in white coats offering a free spray of new Eau Zone. Department stores have an enormous number of lingerie sections. Store designers know that men would rather walk through fire and ice than through a lingerie section, and therefore they are cleverly positioned like electric fences to funnel men into the garden furniture section.

Few would blame you if you believed that shopping trolleys were designed by the same team who gave the Austin Allegro its distinct handling characteristics. In fact the dodgy wheel on shopping trolleys is a deliberate ploy on the part of the supermarkets.

Remember shopping trolleys have no brakes

Off your trolley

I f shopping trolleys went straight as an arrow people would steer straight to the baked beans, pick up a tin and get the hell out. Instead, however hard you try to get straight to the baked beans you end up going via pet foods, personal hygiene, frozen chickens and fresh fruit. On the other hand the dodgy wheel does give you the chance to 'accidentally' bump into dishy looking people in the supermarket.

HANDY HINT: *If you do 'accidentally' bump into someone, make sure it's before you've loaded up with your 210lb Easter turkey, or your first date with this person will be in intensive care where they're having their shattered leg rebuilt.*

There are many, many terrible things that happen in the world but everyone with a shred of conscience agrees that there is no greater evil than shoppers who go through the *'Eight items or less'* check out with fourteen items. If they say that they have *'roughly'* eight items then they should be charged a 50% mark up on every one of their items and when they challenge it they should be told that they shouldn't complain because it's *'roughly'* right. Then they should be flogged.

THE FIVE PEOPLE WHO WILL BE IN FRONT OF YOU AT THE SUPERMARKET CHECKOUT
1   The man with the only unpriced packet of digestives in Northern Europe
2   The long-lost friend of the check out girl
3   The woman who is genetically incapable of deciding between *Good Housekeeping* and *Family Circle*
4   A man with a stocking over his head and a very negative attitude
5   A woman with one tin of cat food and a sack full of coppers

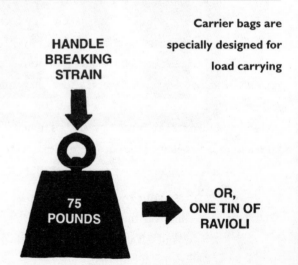

HANDLE BREAKING STRAIN

Carrier bags are specially designed for load carrying

75 POUNDS

OR, ONE TIN OF RAVIOLI

8

WEDDINGS

- Asking for it

- Transport of desire

- Who the hell is that

- Your presents are required

- Last rites

A wedding should get a high priority in the social diary, especially if it's your own. That's because marrying above yourself saves years of grovelling on the cocktail circuit. You'll know when you've married well above yourself when the announcement of your engagement is greeted by a rash of suicides amongst your prospective in-laws.

Asking for it

M en go down on one knee because they know this encourages the rapid formation of a circle of pestilential old people who, in an unexplained spirit of vindictiveness, mutter things like *'Go on dear, he looks lovely.'* For women the trick in avoiding men on one knee is to immediately lie down giving the impression that your suitor is in fact a doctor trying to revive you. If no one is near a good line is, *'What is that you're kneeling in?'* Men who don't think their proposal stands much chance of success should try and slip it in when their partner is saying *'yes'* loudly and repeatedly.

However, if this happens to be when they're in bed with your main rival, you may want to review your options.

WARNING: *Once a proposal is accepted the couple enter a period called* 'engagement'. *This is when rival teams of lawyers are* 'engaged' *to thrash out the pre-nuptial agreement.*

Where you get married is nearly as important as how much money you marry. The two are not unrelated as, like any other retail outlet, Churches have floor limits and you can only reserve an abbey or a cathedral after rigorous credit checks. You can get round this by marrying an abbot or something in that line but remember that vows of celibacy tend to take the edge off honeymoon bliss. Increasingly it has become the fashion to have weddings in places appropriate to the happy couple: amateur sailors married on a yacht, hippies in a stone circle and stockbrokers in an open prison.

Try to steer clear of registry offices. These are faceless little rooms in anonymous government buildings where you can be half way through the ceremony before you realise you're actually in a public inquiry for a new bypass.

CHOOSE YOUR VICAR CAREFULLY

Lemme hear you say *'yeah'*

Transport of desire

There are many old and distinguished customs associated with the journey of the bride to the church. One of these is the right of the bride to keep the groom waiting for about ten minutes. If you want to stress this part of the service, then the most appropriate choice of transport to the church is the Austin Allegro. This allows the bride to be three or four hours late depending on the frequency of local bus services. Often the happy couple decide to leave for their honeymoon in a horse drawn carriage. Remember that horses get as excited as everybody else on the big day and it may be that they have

How to ensure nothing stops you getting to the church on time

to do what horses periodically have to do. At the first sign of this it is vital that anyone with a video camera is immediately knocked to the ground, otherwise the event will be zoomed in on and made the central motif for the whole wedding video.

WARNING: *Most wedding traditions stem from the middle ages when your choice of wedding partners was limited to anything that had survived the Black Death.*

Stag nights were necessary to get the groom so drunk that he wouldn't bolt when the swineherd from the bog lurched up the aisle. Similarly the bride would wear a veil so thick that there would be no chance of focusing on the belching half-wit lined up at the altar.

Today the stag night is a last ditch attempt to persuade the bride-to-be of the merits of single parenthood. It is organised by the best man who is so called because he is best at practical jokes such as getting the groom drunk, giving him a vasectomy and telling him ten years later. In theory the best man is someone the groom can turn to at any time. In practice the groom will turn to the best man once: at the altar when he asks for the ring. The best man will have the ring, but it will be through his nose.

Who the hell is that

I nvitation lists are very important. Write down everyone you've ever met and then cross off anyone who earns less than you. If that includes the person you're engaged to, break it off. Gate-crashers can be a problem at weddings. You can often spend a hard morning turfing out all sorts of undesirables, followed by a hard afternoon explaining to your spouse why their family missed the ceremony. The most unwelcome guest at any wedding is Integral Mike. This is the little microphone on the video camera that records for posterity gems such as, *'Yes he also promised to return my power drill'*.

FIVE WAYS OF ENSURING THAT YOUR MARRIAGE SURVIVES THE FIRST THREE YEARS

1 Keep him waiting at the altar for two and a half years

2 Don't rely on *The Lady* for sex tips

3 Treat your wife with all the loving care and attention that you would any new car

4 Install a team of marriage guidance counsellors in the spare bedroom

5 When you're cleaning your teeth think of all the people you could have married that would have been a lot worse. And then go through them all again, otherwise you won't have cleaned your teeth properly

If you're gate-crashing a wedding yourself, the only time to be careful is when you enter the church and you're asked by the ushers whether you are *'bride'* or *'groom'*. Mutter *'broom'* and let them decide.

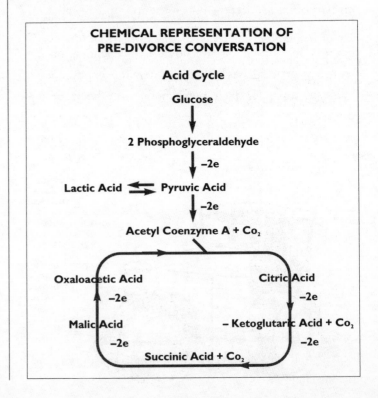

CHEMICAL REPRESENTATION OF PRE-DIVORCE CONVERSATION

Acid Cycle

Glucose

↓

2 Phosphoglyceraldehyde

↓ $-2e$

Lactic Acid ⇌ **Pyruvic Acid**

↓ $-2e$

Acetyl Coenzyme A + CO_2

Oxaloacetic Acid   **Citric Acid**

↑ $-2e$ $-2e$

Malic Acid   **– Ketoglutaric Acid + CO_2**

$-2e$ $-2e$

Succinic Acid + CO_2

Your presents are required

A list of the presents you would like is traditionally left at a department store and of course where you leave it makes a big difference. Your prospective in-laws are not going to be too impressed if they have to thumb through your list at Millets. What you put on your list is a good way of telling your guests what sort of married life you're planning. Therefore, even though you may be desperate for them, don't ask for a roll of lino and a steel bucket.

DON'T FORGET: *Include things like quail egg poachers and polo mallets which you'll never need but which can, with a bit of imagination, be pressed into service on the allotment.*

On the other hand if as a guest you are forced to choose from one of these lists, pick something like a 700 piece dinner service and buy one plate. Top up the gift with something that you feel reflects on the marriage; for example a book of Legal Aid vouchers.

During the actual service the most poignant moment is during the wedding vows when the groom reveals to the waiting world that his middle name is Percy. Tradition dictates that this is greeted with loud, prolonged and raucous laughter.

What to wear at the altar is a very big decision indeed. There are literally thousands of designs available, from cute little off-the-shoulder numbers to ruched waterfalls of crepe de Chine. And it's not just vicars who have to look good. Brides traditionally wear something white in memory of their virginity.

6 POINT WEDDING LIST FOR UNSUCCESSFUL MARRIAGE

5-GALLON DUSTBIN
3-GAL 'DIXIE'
NYLON SIEVE
WOODEN SPOON
RUBBER TUBING
FLAGONS
ASSORTED FUNNELS
A BLANKET

Last rites

On leaving the church or registry office it is traditional to throw rice. Relatives and close friends are entitled to throw special egg-fried rice. Confetti is also most welcome. If none is to hand make use of any available churchyard debris such as grass cuttings, service books and headstones. This is also the time when the official photographer makes his unpleasant presence felt. He has two functions: one is to provide a jarring sartorial note with his nasty brown suit and the other is to ruin the atmosphere by herding groups of relatives together who for the last fifty years have had a blood feud. Shortly before they leave on their honeymoon, the newly-weds' car is decorated with congratulatory messages sprayed on with

THE MOST COMMON REASONS CITED FOR DIVORCE
1 Marriage
2 Children bearing an uncanny resemblance to a previous *'long-forgotten'* boyfriend
3 The desire to turn your in-laws into out-laws
4 Contempt bred of familiarity
5 A burning desire to turn over a large part of one's personal wealth to lawyers

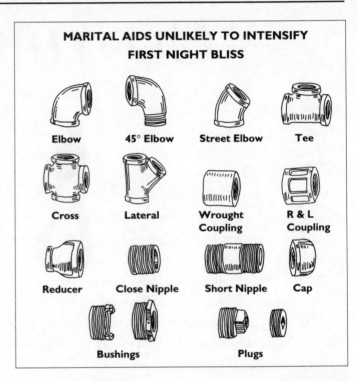

MARITAL AIDS UNLIKELY TO INTENSIFY FIRST NIGHT BLISS

Elbow · 45° Elbow · Street Elbow · Tee

Cross · Lateral · Wrought Coupling · R & L Coupling

Reducer · Close Nipple · Short Nipple · Cap

Bushings · Plugs

paint stripper. It is also customary to attach a string of clanking metal objects to be towed behind their car. These objects are traditionally removed from the engine. If all these traditions are adhered to, by the end of the day the couple will be well and truly *'happy'*.

9

CLOTHING

- Off the cuff

- Off Savile Row

- Off to work we go

- Off the shoulder

- Off the beaten track

I f you are what you wear, then a lot of people would appear to be mobile laundry baskets. That's because in the morning, unless you have a team of image consultants on 24-hour standby, you're more than likely to pull on the first thing that's not past its smell-by date. This simply won't do if you're hoping to have any sort of social impact. Clothes should be making statements such as *'Yves worked late on this one'*. At the same time clothes should at all costs be avoiding statements such as *'I'm an easy-iron, drip-dry, flame-retardant kind of guy.'*

Off the cuff

F|or men, the whole business of clothing is now a lot simpler than it was in Victorian times. Everyone from navvies upwards wore a suit and therefore the only way to rise above the herd was to have more pieces than anyone else. You couldn't start to make an impression with anything less than a twelve piece suit.

You could also beef up your image with a whole range of accessories. In the average office a lot of mileage could be had from a well cut spat. Shirts had to have as many bits removable as possible with detachable collars, cuffs, tails, sleeves etc. In fact most mornings you had to start with a pile of cloth and just a general idea of what a shirt looked like.

WARNING: *Suits today are a lot simpler with a popular choice being the 'off-the-peg' suit. This is*

THE FIVE ITEMS OF CLOTHING THAT CAUSE THE MOST MERRIMENT AMONGST REMOTE AMAZONIAN TRIBES ON FIRST SEEING THEM		
1 Panties	3 Ribbed tights	5 Arsenal scarf
2 Pith helmet	4 Cummerbund	

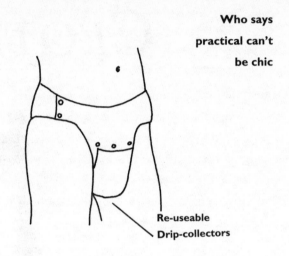

Who says practical can't be chic

Re-useable
Drip-collectors

generally made from a frightening combination of unnatural fibres and is excellent if you enjoy little streaks of blue lightning flickering around you every time you walk across a synthetic carpet.

These suits do fit, but not everywhere at once. They also come in an exciting range of colours from blue-grey to grey-blue. These suits will of course last a lifetime, but only if you die shortly after buying one. For anyone with a modicum of self-respect, off-the-peg suits are best left *on* the peg.

Off Savile Row

The thing to go for is a tailor made suit. These are also called bespoke suits because after you get the bill you can't speak. The advantage of these suits is that because they are tailor made they can be adjusted to hide certain personal irregularities. For example, if you are an extremely wealthy but overweight businessman, the pinstripe of your suit can be subtly tailored to lead the eye away from the paunch, around the side of the body and down to the wallet. Similarly, people who carry weapons find this facility particularly useful. A well-cut Savile Row suit will smooth away the tell-tale bulges of, say, a multiple rocket launcher.

If you think looking good is for poofs and you regard your body as nothing more than a holdall for your vital organs, then the suit for you is the shell suit. The shell suit is the Exxon Valdez of the clothing world, a total and unmitigated disaster that does untold damage to the environment. Should senior members of the Royal family take to wearing shell suits for major state occasions, then it would clearly be time to borrow a couple of guillotines from the French. A typical accessory for the shell suit is the bum bag. This is a sort of pregnant belt which many people choose to wear round the front as a sort of Euro-sporran.

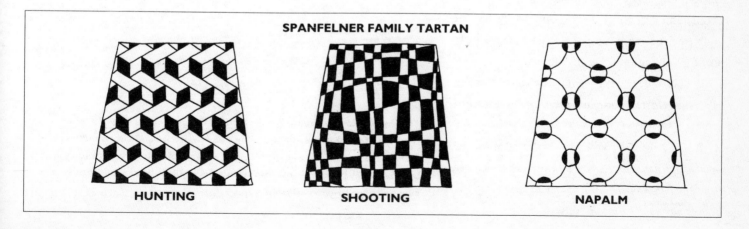

SPANFELNER FAMILY TARTAN

HUNTING **SHOOTING** **NAPALM**

Off to work we go

I f you wear a suit day in, day out the only chance you get to express yourself is through your tie. Many men take this opportunity to make bold and daring statements such as *'I think my tie would be happier as a sock.'*

WARNING: *Windsor knots are so called because when you've tied one properly you tend to sound like Prince Charles.*

Club ties are an important item for the social climber. If you don't actually belong to any school, university or regiment worth shouting about, you can cover all the options by having your own tie made up with an impressive little motif involving books, guns and whips.

If you're ever asked what the tie represents say, *'I could tell you, but then I'd have to kill you'.*

REMEMBER: *If you've actually been to one of these institutions, you'll know that having the Old Etonian tie isn't nearly as important as having the Old Etonian body stocking.*

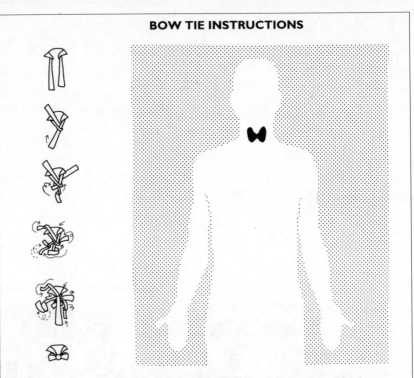

BOW TIE INSTRUCTIONS

The thyroid gland is situated at the front of the neck. It consists of 2 lobes at the sides of the trachea, connected by a narrow isthmus. Cells within the gland secrete a substance called thyroglobulin, whose molecules are chemically split by enzymes into the 2 hormones thyroxine and triiodothyronine. Place your bow-tie above the thyroid gland.

Off the shoulder

F or social impact, women are expected to wear designer clothing from the big fashion houses. However, one of the disadvantages of designer clothing is that the labels are on the inside. What they need to do is build in some Littlewoods V-neck jumper technology so that the label is always pinging out at the back.

REMEMBER: *Once you have forked out for a designer item, you obviously want to make sure people notice it. Leave the electronic security tag on and then spend a lot of time hanging around airports and hospitals, and anywhere else they have sensitive equipment you can set off.*

When it comes to your choice of what to wear, colour is obviously of vital importance. For example, if you are wearing a powder blue cravat, your chance of social success could hinge on the minute aesthetic of a delicate salmon pink or a more perky FT pink for the matching lederhosen.

As social success often hinges on how successfully you can get your feet in various doors, choice of footwear assumes particular importance. You are either of the Clint Eastwood school of footwear where you have one favourite pair that you wear in bed, in the bath and in your coffin, or you are of the Imelda Marcos school where you have 5000 pairs of shoes, none of which quite suit the occasion. Whatever school you subscribe to, make sure you obey the three golden rules of footwear: a shoe should never have a tongue longer than that of its owner, it should never have a welt wide enough for a mountain goat to stand on; and no one ever made friends by wearing a shoe with an integral sockette.

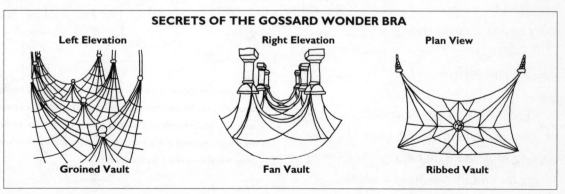

SECRETS OF THE GOSSARD WONDER BRA

Left Elevation	Right Elevation	Plan View
Groined Vault	Fan Vault	Ribbed Vault

Off the beaten track

O bviously if you're socially successful you should have the sort of walk-in wardrobe that would be of considerable interest to the Rambler's Association. On the other hand, don't despair if your entire wardrobe can be displayed on three hangers.

REMEMBER: *You can make large social strides with the intelligent use of accessories such as earrings.*

Think of the class exuded by a couple of cut glass decanter stoppers hanging from your lobes, and after you've had a think choose something else.

If your clothing really is no help, try carrying a cane with a silver knob. People are bound to be impressed by this, especially when you've whacked them with it a couple of times.

Taking your clothes off is as important as putting them on. When you go to bed there are complex rules about what to take off first in order to get the maximum possible effect. These are common sense and only an idiot would try and get his underpants off before removing his coat. Finally, before you put on your pyjamas, ask yourself whether you would be ashamed to wear them in the presence of the Royal family. You never know your luck.

FIVE ITEMS WITHOUT WHICH A GENTLEMAN'S WARDROBE IS INCOMPLETE	
1	A door
2	Suspicious damp smell
3	Junior tennis racket
4	Packet of three, well past their sell-by date
5	Dubious literature

Tailors are trained to ignore mid-fitting erections

NIGHTLIFE

F or the majority of people the most common form of nightlife is sleeping. In fact this is a logical extension of all other forms of nightlife as they are all geared to finishing the night in bed, preferably with someone else.

Cock's crow

P eople with an active nightlife get a lot of media attention but there is an equally active arena of social life that gets hardly any. If hardened night owls didn't feel so utterly wretched when they slunk back home at 5 o'clock in the morning, they might notice it; its called *early morning life*. The only requirement for membership of this exclusive club is the ability to say *dawn really is the best part of the day* without any trace of irony. These are people who greet you at breakfast

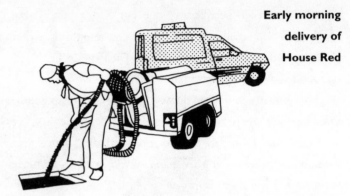

Early morning delivery of House Red

with the news that in the four or five hours of glorious sunshine since dawn they have remodelled the garden, run a half-marathon and completed next years tax returns. The only good thing about these sort of people is that they have to go to bed shortly after *Eastenders*.

One reason why more people don't opt for the early morning life option is that you have precious little chance of getting a stiff drink at six in the morning unless you have a special arrangement with the milkman. Nightlife cruises gently along on a river of alcohol. People drink for three reasons; to forget, to remember and to forget what they remember.

WARNING: *Remember that drinking isn't funny or clever or grown-up, it just makes you feel that way.*

DANCING: AVOID WARM UP DRINK

Get beside her with rosé

*T*he difference between a wine bar and a pub is that when you stroll into a wine bar you're unlikely to see someone with a glass of Chateauneuf Du Pape in his hand, surrounded by six of his mates chanting, *'Down in one, down in one, down in one.'* Down in three or four, possibly. Wine bars are where sophisticated, educated people meet for intelligent and informed conversation and the chance of a shag. *When ordering in a wine bar, you'll make more of an impression if you don't start your order with 'A pint of...'*

Of course, the atmosphere can suddenly turn nasty anywhere where alcohol is consumed. Wine bar fights can be among the dirtiest and most costly. You won't know anything has happened until suddenly someone drops his business card on your table and says *'You'll be hearing from my solicitor.'*

In restaurants there is an enormous amount of snobbery attached to wine, and most people are very nervous of the wine list, especially when the wine waiter is breathing down his enormous nose at you. Which is why the house red is still easily the most popular wine and why Chateau de House in the industrial area of Northern France is by far and away the most prosperous.

4 signs that you've had too much to drink

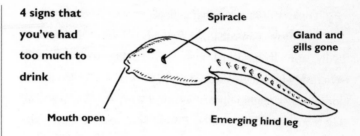

Spiracle

Gland and gills gone

Mouth open

Emerging hind leg

In the old days couples used to go to the cinema to court. Nowadays they just go for a snog. When couples get sick and tired of sitting at home in the dark watching mindless violence on television they often decide to ring the changes by sitting in the dark watching mindless violence at the cinema. The one drawback about the cinema is the computer booking system that tells you exactly where to sit even in an empty cinema. If you're the first person in the cinema the computer gives you exactly the same seat as it gave to the person who opened his toffee popcorn upside down in the matinee. The second person gets the seat right next to you, unless he happens to be over six foot four and then he gets the seat directly in front of you. The third person gets the ticket for the exact same seat you moved to in order to get away from the second person.

Public houses for the public spirited

P ubs are the open plan offices of the black economy. More business gets done in a short evening session in the pub than a long day in the office. That's why people who say 'I don't drink at lunch because I can't work in the afternoon' are missing the point. If they went down the pub at lunch they would get so much business done that they wouldn't need to work in the afternoon. Pub food has improved in leaps and bounds since they had the catering consultants from the hospitals in.

WARNING: *Pubs that advertise 'Hot and Cold Food' generally serve microwaved lasagne that is scalding on the outside and still frozen on the inside.*

Of course, some people go to pubs to drink. These are the sad *'regulars'* with their pewter mugs hanging behind the bar, specially engraved with the name Alan. Alan will come in, call the landlord by his first name and get served within seconds, even if you've been waiting to order since shortly after opening time. Alan will also have his favourite chair which is completely unmarked. If you make the mistake of sitting in it, fifteen regulars will treat you as if you're hot in from jumping up and down on the grave of Alan's mother.

If you're a member of the upper crust, the place to spend one's evenings is at a charity ball. These are where the cream of English society, the freakish products of centuries of inbreeding, gather to select partners in order to further aggravate their congenital deficiencies. On the dance floor, young well bred men crash around with a hellish disregard for the beat, every so often lurching clumsily backwards to rip a gaping hole in eight months worth of hand-stitched chiffon ball dress and then apologise by throwing up. At the end of the evening a small quiet man with a tin picks his way through the minefield of vomiting Arabellas and raises £42.14 for Somalia.

Mine's a sweet sherry

Being served quickly is all about confidence

Clubs 1

*T*here are several different types of nightclub and it's important not to confuse them. Before you begin an evening, choose carefully between a rave in a large warehouse and The Royal British Legion's Darby and Joan night.

USEFUL TIP: *If you are wearing a regimental tie, your name is Darby and your idea of a designer drug is Sanatogen, then why not give the warehouse a try?*

People go to nightclubs ostensibly to meet people, which is a bit odd because once you're inside you can't see them, hear them or speak to them. In a nightclub there is an ancient tradition which dictates that the ladies put their handbags down and dance round them. For a while there was a tradition where men would throw their wallets on the floor and dance round them, but this petered out for some reason.

Dancing is a very good way of impressing the opposite sex, because if you are a good mover on the dance floor it suggests that you might be rather impressive between the sheets. That's why when you're on the dance floor, spinning on your head isn't to be recommended. If women wanted spinning in their sex life, they would go to bed

with a tumble dryer. If your dancing can best be described as a robot collapsing at the end of a marathon, just hang around by the bar looking tough but sensitive.

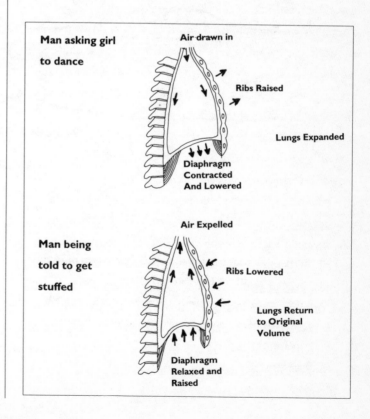

Man asking girl to dance

Air drawn in

Ribs Raised

Lungs Expanded

Diaphragm Contracted And Lowered

Man being told to get stuffed

Air Expelled

Ribs Lowered

Lungs Return to Original Volume

Diaphragm Relaxed and Raised

Clubs 2

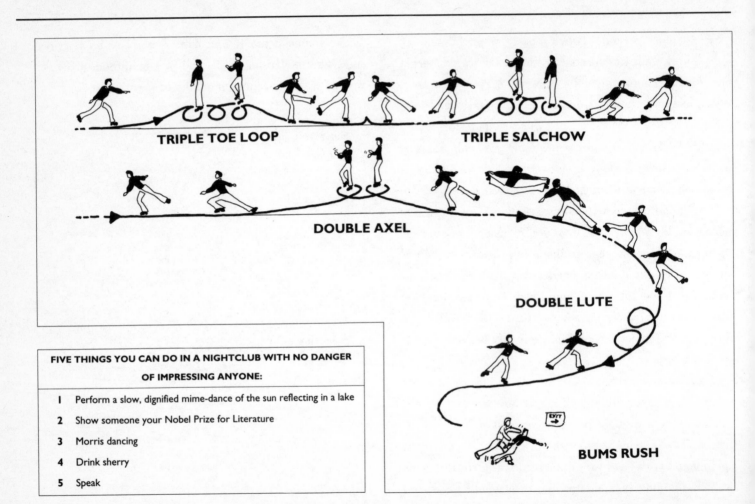

TRIPLE TOE LOOP

TRIPLE SALCHOW

DOUBLE AXEL

DOUBLE LUTE

BUMS RUSH

FIVE THINGS YOU CAN DO IN A NIGHTCLUB WITH NO DANGER OF IMPRESSING ANYONE:

1   Perform a slow, dignified mime-dance of the sun reflecting in a lake

2   Show someone your Nobel Prize for Literature

3   Morris dancing

4   Drink sherry

5   Speak

Greeters

B|ouncers are in fact highly trained individuals who can respond to a whole range of medical and social emergencies. The fact that their solution is always to try and rip somebody's head off is neither here nor there. Bouncers love getting tips. Try giving this one, *'Don't try to lick the blades on a mixer before you've turned it off.'* Bouncers always dress up very smartly often in dinner jackets and part of their job, quite rightly, is to turn people away who are wearing jeans. Of course there is a way round this if you turn up wearing jeans. Simply point out that you would like to go inside and they are standing outside, so why don't you just swap trousers.

FIVE UNLIKELY THINGS FOR A BOUNCER TO SAY

1   Please don't be so confrontational

2   That's less than my job's worth

3   You can go in, love, because you're rather plain looking

4   Sorry, single men only

5   Well if you promise you're a boy scout, you can keep that nine inch knife

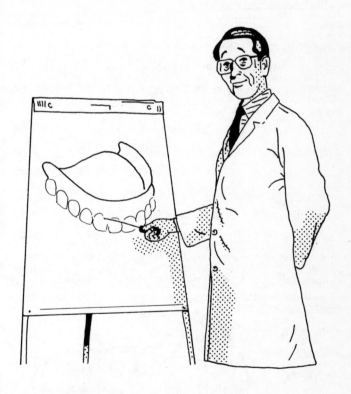

Tooth most commonly lost in confrontation with bouncers

Going home

W|hen you stagger home just before the dawn you generally feel on the point of throwing up if you haven't already done so. That's when the devil takes possession of you and you suddenly decide that the best possible cure would be a kebab. Kebab vans are an attempt sponsored by the Greek government to pay us back for us walking away with the Elgin marbles.

Of course, if you think walking home late at night is dangerous, you can try taking an unlicensed minicab. This is just as dangerous but slightly quicker. Minicabs are driven by people who are only doing it to earn enough money to pay for their driving lessons. If you ever get to where you're supposed to be going, never give a minicab driver a twenty pound note. Not only will they not have change, but their English will also suddenly deteriorate.

This is not an unlicensed minicab. Insist on a dodgy Japanese banger

FOOD CHAIN

74

11

COLLEGE

Do Not
Disturb

☐ *Tutorials*

☐ *Sage stuffing*

☐ *Discussion*

☐ *Born again Christians*

☐ *Graduation*

*E*ducation is what separates the unemployed labourer from the unemployed managing director. If people knew how awful work was they would never leave full-time education. In fact the only reason for not extending the time you spend in education is an allergy to paper. Even then, an English degree is still a viable option.

Tutorials

Y ou can spend three years at college and not sit through a single lecture. What you can't do is avoid tutorials. For most students, tutorials are a form of coitus interruptus. If you have to go to one, don't arrive half an hour early. This causes embarrassment for tutors, who like as not will be lying naked on a black rug worshipping the devil or watching video re-runs of *Blind Date*. Nor should you arrive half an hour late, fanning the still wet essay with the pages of the book from which it has just been copied. Arrive bang on time. The college bell will chime the hour; wait until the last stroke and then announce your arrival with one firm knock. A second after they have said *'come in'*, knock again, only this time slightly louder; then once more like the Angel of Death. When they ask you why you knocked three times, tell them that you didn't in fact knock at all. If they begin to suspect that they are losing their senses this will help considerably when you come to read out your essay.

Don't slump into the nearest seat. Instead, say to your tutor *'Do you mind if I pace up and down it helps me think.'* As their job is ostensibly to encourage you to think, they can't really object, so you can spend a whole tutorial circling round behind their chair, darting in and out of the furniture and generally having a good time. Alternatively, if your tutor is sitting next to the fire, go and sit behind his desk. If this is successful you can try answering the phone and saying *'I'm afraid he can't talk right now, he's getting dressed.'*

THE FAMOUS FIRST LINES OF LECTURES THAT SECURED THE DISMISSAL OF THE ACADEMICS THAT DELIVERED THEM

1 English should be about the enjoyment of great literature

2 The main purpose of Chemistry is to allow students to manufacture their own hallucinogens

3 History is about the English and how they moulded the world in their own image

4 Better men than I have been asking the same questions in philosophy and have never come up with any satisfactory answers, so there's precious little chance of me contributing anything useful

5 The immutable laws of physics can't really be understood except when one is naked

Sage Stuffing

D on't bring your essay in a soiled Kwik Save carrier bag. What you should do is open a briefcase, take out a fat file with lots of indexes and dividers and carefully select this week's essay from a lot of others as if you'd done them all on your year off. Write on one side of the paper only and give yourself huge margins and treble spacing. For every sheet you write, accidentally include five loose blank sheets. When your tutor sees you heaving out a great fat wodge of paper they will think they are in for a mammoth swatty essay and gently slip their brains into neutral. When you conclude with a flourish thirty seconds later they will naturally assume they had fallen asleep. Tell them they groaned something about Baroness Thatcher and deep cuts in their sleep.

Unread books make useful bookends for other unread books

Excessive masturbation is no excuse for failing to produce an essay

If your tutor is the annoying type who insists on listening to the overnight drivel you have produced, reading your essay out will be made considerably easier if when writing it you have already rendered it tutor-proof. You can start with a quotation from Durkheim. No tutor has read him/her so you can just make one up.

REMEMBER: *useful words to include in an essay are* counter-factual, post-rationalisation *and* lunch (*this last one always sets their mind wandering*).
Foreign quotations are also good unless your tutor happens to be foreign. Never, ever mention the word plagiarism in an essay.

Discussion

*I*f tutors have the annoying habit of interrupting you in full flow to make trivial points, look them sternly in the eye and say *'I'm just coming to that'*. You never will of course, but the wait will so unsettle them that they will miss the rest of your essay and forget what it was you were supposed to be coming to.

WARNING: *The post-essay discussion is the most important part of the tutorial, as all your good work can be destroyed in one comment. There are three basic rules:*

a) keep your mouth shut

b) if asked a question, faint

c) if you have to say something, make it, *'Didn't you cover this in your excellent book?'*

The end of the tutorial is also a critical time. Firstly, suggest that the tutorial should end; *'I'm sorry, I must stop you there. You've been moderately entertaining, but I really must go and play tennis now.'* Then shake hands. This always throws them. It means either you're leaving for good, or they'll soon be leaving for good because you've unearthed the act of unspeakable depravity that doubtless they've been involved in. Finally throw some loose change in the pot, take a volume from their bookcase and saunter out of the room leaving the door wide open.

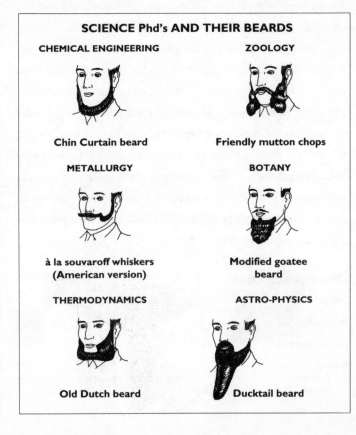

SCIENCE Phd's AND THEIR BEARDS

CHEMICAL ENGINEERING
Chin Curtain beard

ZOOLOGY
Friendly mutton chops

METALLURGY
à la souvaroff whiskers (American version)

BOTANY
Modified goatee beard

THERMODYNAMICS
Old Dutch beard

ASTRO-PHYSICS
Ducktail beard

Born again Christians

A t college there are certain select clubs where like minded individuals meet together on a regular basis *'to get more out of life'*. The most chilling of these is the Christian Union. If there's one thing that puts the fear of God into the average student, it's a born again Christian. Born again students are branded by two grossly unstudentlike characteristic: firstly they always seem to have a brand new car; and secondly, they have breakfast at eight o' clock (in the morning). In Student Union meetings up and down the country, there are regular attempts to curb the Christian Union menace, by calls for the re-introduction of born-again lions in born-again amphitheatres. These motions are always sponsored by the Rugby Club with some passing interest from those studying classical history.

What you wear at college says more about you than you could ever say yourself. If you wear the college scarf you are studying chemistry, bio-chemistry or chemical engineering. If you wear the college tie you are studying agriculture. If you wear the college cravat you are the offspring of a third world dictator and it doesn't matter what you study. And if you wear the college ale in big splodges down whatever else you are wearing, it's highly unlikely that you are studying anything. If you wear a brown corduroy suit, you are either the nerdiest student ever, or a senior and very distinguished academic. The tragedy is that these two breeds are not unrelated.

WARNING FLAGS AT COLLEGE BARS

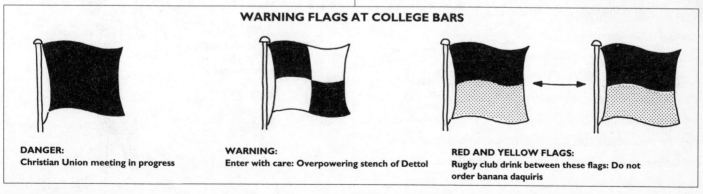

DANGER:
Christian Union meeting in progress

WARNING:
Enter with care: Overpowering stench of Dettol

RED AND YELLOW FLAGS:
Rugby club drink between these flags: Do not order banana daquiris

Graduation

G raduation is an elaborate ceremony put on for the benefit of parents, who are given a day's leave from their debtor's prisons. At the ceremony you are recognised as having successfully converted an enormous quantity of beer into an equally enormous overdraft and you are given the first piece of paper you have seen for three years.

The Chancellor says something in Latin which translates as *'If I ever see you here again, I'll call the police'* and you are then free to sign on.

THE CHOSEN PROFESSIONS OF BRITAIN'S ENGINEERING GRADUATES			
1	Financial services	6	Pastry chef
2	Marketing	7	Trichologist
3	Choreography	8	Male nurse
4	Backing singer	9	Beautician
5	Professional bowls	10	Fabric designer

COLLECTING DEGREES

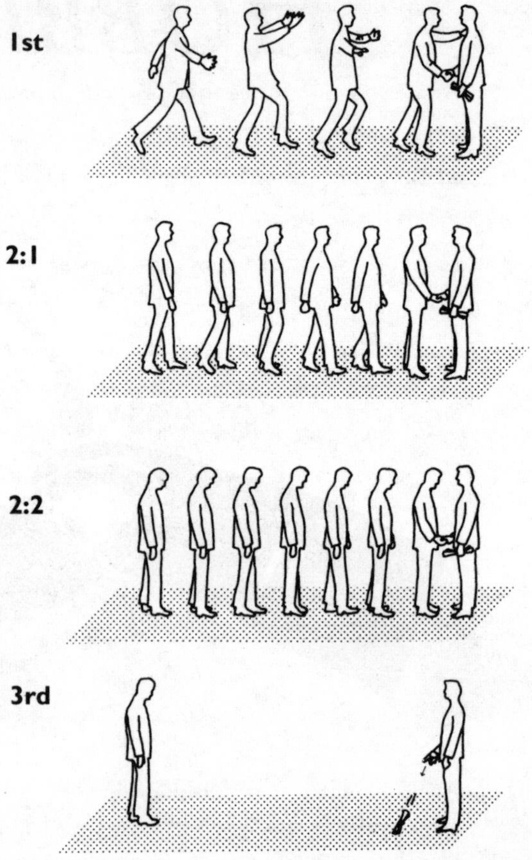

1st

2:1

2:2

3rd

12

HOBBIES

- Bits and bobs

- Cheese and wine

- Train gang

- Birds and nerds

- Needles and fins

H aving a hobby is an admission that you have a lot of time to spare which means you are either a convict, a Member of the European Parliament, or a premature ejaculator or all three.

Bits and bobs

Whenever you come across something really rather nasty and you're trying to scrape it off with a spatula, remember that someone, somewhere collects it and has many others like it. Collecting things is a bizarre, inexplicable ritual. If you've got a rusting industrial boiler in the back garden, your neighbours will soon be reporting you to the council. If, on the other hand, you've got seventeen rusting industrial boilers in the back garden, your neighbours will be leaning over the fence saying things like, *'That's quite a collection you've got there, Bert.'*

At one time many people used to collect Green Shield stamps. If you spent the equivalent of £20,000 on groceries you could fill up a book and exchange it for a small green shield. This was very popular in the sixties and seventies. But so was Harold Wilson.

If you were young at that time you could either collect boils on the back of your neck or cards from packets of tea. If you went for the tea card option, the problem was that you could never get the last card in your *'Saga of Ships'* album because some freak distribution accident meant that a small area around Bridlington had been swamped with HMS Dreadnought. Coin collecting starts when your parents return from Belgium, empty their loose change into a pot and say this is your hobby. You then spend three years happily cataloguing and sorting your collection until one day it disappears and you get a postcard from your sister in Antwerp.

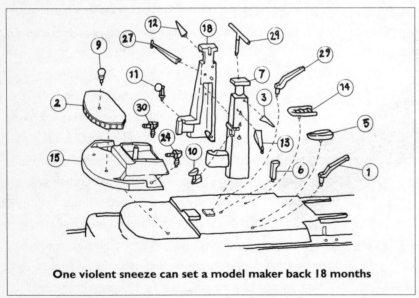

One violent sneeze can set a model maker back 18 months

Cheese and wine

A number of curious hobbies involve going to enormous lengths to make things at home that you can easily buy at the shops. You'll know this sort of person when they say *'We make our own toothpaste'* and smile at you with a crumbling mass of blackened scorched teeth. Home brewing is also unnecessarily popular. This involves taking obscure articles of domestic waste such as carpet fluff, loose plaster or limescale, and fermenting it in the bathroom cabinet. After waiting ten years you open it and quietly pour it down the toilet. Alternatively after seven weeks your house blows up. Many home brewers are

---

FIVE HOBBIES THAT ARE A LOT MORE POPULAR THAN YOU WOULD HAVE THOUGHT UNLESS YOU'RE ONE OF THE PEOPLE THAT DOES THEM:

1   Collecting paper clips, straightening them out and fashioning home-made orthodontic appliances

2   Waiting quietly for Mr Right to walk up the path and ring the front doorbell

3   Collecting small pieces of paper with *'I promise to pay the bearer'* on them

4   Fashioning mounds of accumulated ear wax into busts of jazz legends

5   Hanging round dentist's waiting rooms on the off chance that there is some spare drilling time

---

currently being held under the Prevention of Terrorism Act.

Since the decline of shipbuilding, our largest surviving manufacturing industry is the production of delightful porcelain figurines that capture a forgotten era of romance and elegance. These are obviously collected as an investment as they are only issued in special limited editions of 400,000. Each one is lovingly hand painted by craftsmen and women in cardigans and half-moon glasses. And when they've lovingly finished the first two they lovingly sub-contract some Filipino child labour to finish off the rest.

Home made fudge-making is a demanding and fiercely competitive hobby

A   NOT B   NOT C

Train gang

F or most men sex is a sublimation of their obsession with trains. All train spotters have books of numbers which they tick off when they have seen a train. When you have filled out a whole book you have to do it again, but standing on one leg. Train spotters now like to video trains when they roar through the station. This is incredibly exciting and means that when they get home they can watch something blurred flash past, followed by spinning sky and a close-up of the platform, where they tripped over a luggage trolley.

FACT: *A popular hobby amongst train drivers is spotting train spotters. You get one point for a soiled parka, two points for a tartan thermos, and ten points if at the last moment you pull your train into the platform farthest away from where they are all gathered.*

VIRTUAL TRAIN SPOTTING

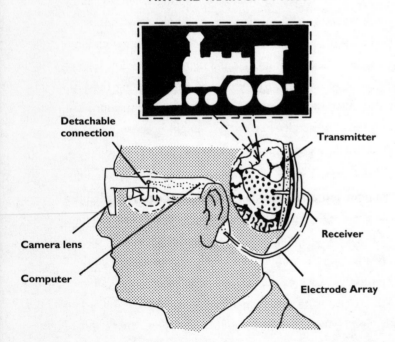

Detachable connection

Transmitter

Camera lens

Receiver

Computer

Electrode Array

ROLL OF HONOUR FOR THOSE WHO DIED WHILE STAMP COLLECTING:	
Mr Leon Tucker	Mr Ronald 'Perf' Peters
Mr Barry Decker	Mr Harry Edwards
Mr Frank Horseman	Mr Eldon Melchett
Mrs Yvonne Grenshaw	Miss Sarah Mumby
Mr David Smith	Mr Paul Vale

Birds and nerds

T he qualification for being a bird spotter is a big pair of binoculars, an underdeveloped sense of the absurd, and the personality of a bucket. When a rare bird is spotted anywhere in Britain, urgent phone calls alert birdwatchers up and down the country. Senior civil servants slip quietly out of their offices, rush off to remote corners of the country and lie face down in freezing bogs. Naturally, when junior civil servants find this out, there are a lot of hoax calls.

WARNING: *When bird spotters converge on a sighting, they are sometimes tailed by equally keen, rival hobbyists such as egg collectors and taxidermists, and scuffling can often break out.*

Rambling also takes place in the country. This is where people dress up like Scott of the Antarctic and walk round a local field in a pack. They then clog up a local pub and test each other on the country code.

Tinkering with their car accounts for 90% of the time that men tell Cosmopolitan surveys they spend locked in carnal ecstasy. There are two crucial stages: the first is taking all the bits out and laying them on the lawn; the second is rediscovering them in the spring when you mow your lawn. You then develop a whole new hobby of lawnmower maintenance. A traditional hobby for children is to put a stick insect in a jar and then drop a whole load of twigs in, so they can have hours of fun watching the little bugger work himself into a lather of sexual frustration. The stick insect generally has the last laugh, because what the kid thought were twigs were in fact a number of the stick insect's close friends.

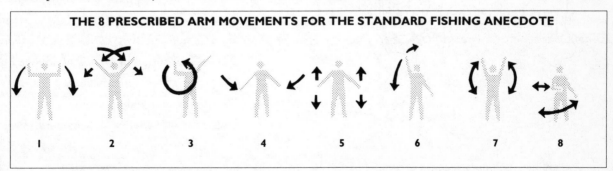

THE 8 PRESCRIBED ARM MOVEMENTS FOR THE STANDARD FISHING ANECDOTE

1   2   3   4   5   6   7   8

Needles and fins

K nitting is extremely therapeutic and is great for relieving tension. That's why so many captains of industry and deep sea divers do it. It has been estimated that if the entire national output of knitting was made into one giant jumper, St. Paul's Cathedral would fit comfortably inside, although it would probably be a bit long in the nave. Tropical fish, like knitting, are also considered excellent for relaxation. That's why you often see them in dentists' waiting rooms. Curiously, in tropical dentists' waiting rooms, a murky tank full of English pond slime, frog spawn and minature shopping trolleys is considered the ultimate in relaxation.

Recently the two best selling non-fiction titles in America were *1001 Ways to Please your Lover* and *More and Better Sex*. At the same time the number one book in Britain was the *Royal Horticultural Society's Encyclopaedia*

Fish unlikely to induce feelings of tranquility in you

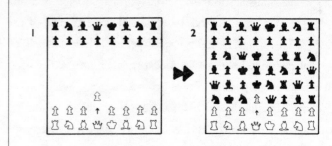

The correct response to the Al-Rashid opening is the Schwartzkopf defense

of Gardening. In both countries, beds are where vigorous activity is undertaken in the planting of seeds, but in Britain this leads to the sweet pea. The reason why so many people garden in this country must be because the weather is so good. The last thing people want to do when there is a steady cold drizzle falling is to be cooped up in the warm when they could just as easily be up to their neck in freezing mud planting cabbage bulbs, or whatever it is you plant to get cabbages. A lot of gardeners bang on about how marvellous home grown vegetables are, but what they don't tell you is that for every pound of home grown potatoes you dig up, you have to plunge the fork through your foot at least twice.

13

OFFICE

Z Z Z Z Z Z Z Z Z Z Z

O ne of the reasons so many people work in offices is because they apply for jobs that say *'Executive Opportunity'* when really what they offer is *'Series of Irritating Chores'*. The office is no different from the rest of the world, and if you ever suspect that the classless society extends to the office try ignoring the tradesman's entrance of a private bank and striding into reception with a tray of fish.

Blowing your job

Getting a job in the first place requires passing the interview. This isn't difficult if you follow a few simple rules. Interviews start with the knock on the door. Lesson one therefore is to make sure you knock on the right door. Getting all psyched up for the big entrance and then disappearing into the broom cupboard is no way to start a career in high finance.

Once inside, the next thing to do is to close the door, but on no account should you turn your back while doing this. They will have seen your face and the split second your back is turned is enough for the chairman to raise one eyebrow and for six members of the panel to put a little cross against your name.

The next vital thing not to do is sit down. If you have watched any television at all, you will know that really top business people take their jackets off and stand, hands clasped behind their back, staring out of the window. So, hang your jacket on the chair and make for that window. If they do not offer you the job on the strength of that, then they are probably not the sort of company you want to work for anyway.

USEFUL TIP: *If you must sit down, try taking the chair and pulling it right up to the desk where the chairman is sitting. He will be so affronted that he will instinctively move his own chair back. Then he will be the one sitting in the lonely chair in the middle of nowhere.*

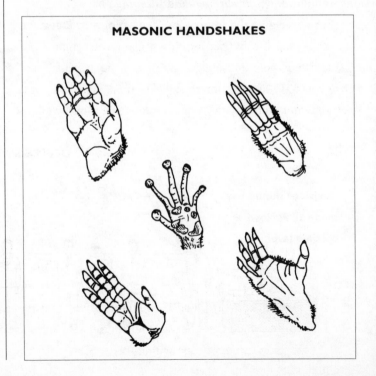

MASONIC HANDSHAKES

CVs

A quick word on application forms. Most sections can be adequately filled in by gross exaggeration and good old-fashioned lying, but one section needs special care – that marked *'interests'*. Do not put down *'walking'* or *'reading'* as everyone does that and you might as well put down *'breathing'* and *'sleeping'*.

But never give the impression that you do in fact have an interesting life by putting down glamorous things like scuba diving, polo and bungee jumping. If the panel suspect that you have a more interesting life than theirs they are certainly not going to give you an interesting job as well.

USEFUL TIP: *Put something interesting like horse breaking which of course you don't do. When they inevitably ask you about horse breaking just tell them that it was a typo and that 'horse' should have read 'wind'.*

Company car parks are a social climbers dream with special places marked out for *'Chairman'*, *'Director'* etc. You can guarantee your own spot with a sign saying *'Office Nerd'*. On the other hand you can have the Chairman's spot by replacing his sign with *'Official Receiver'*.

OFFICE SUBSIDIARITY

Decisions should be made at the lowest possible level

Getting yourself to work

A lot of people commute on trains, the idea being that you freshen up for work by spending half an hour bent double with an umbrella jabbed in your groin and your head wedged in a Hell's Angel's armpit.

To create more of an impact you may prefer to pull on a pair of lycra underpants, jump on a mountain bike and cycle to work. The one drawback with this is that you can find yourself half way through a high level meeting before you realise that you've still got a polystyrene mushroom on your head.

The most common cause of lateness in the office is the 9 o'clock start time. If your boss insists on having breakfast meetings, creep through the door in your dressing gown with a variety pack of cereals. Every time someone tries to get the meeting underway say 'OK, *who's taken the Coco Pops?'*

If you live more than 40 miles from the office walking to work isn't necessarily the healthy option

Desk job

*I*n business life you are judged on how big your desk is. Aim for one so big that no one can get the door of your office open. The advantage of big desks is that in the time it takes someone to walk round the side you can drop some weighty looking documents over your copy of *Hello*.

USEFUL TIP: *Another good thing to have is a complex executive toy that, whenever someone interferes with it, collapses in a heap on your desk. No-one's going to ask you to work late after they've destroyed your toy.*

Once you've got your big desk the next step to success is to avoid any form of decision. If ever you think you may be facing one, simply adjourn the meeting, commission research and employ an outside consultancy. If worst comes to worst hide under your desk.

If you don't have a personal hygiene problem you are unlikely to be any good at computers. Don't be bullied by pointy headed computer swats. Insert a special programme that says, whatever key they press, '*You have crashed the entire network. Please clear your desk and collect your P45*'. Remember every computer has an integral labour saving device. It's called the on/off switch. Switch it off and go home.

**Dress in the City may have become less formal,
but the bowler hat is still compulsory**

Fuse blowers

A void telephones. They seem terribly simple until a client calls to place an order that will guarantee your company's future into the next century. Three hours after trying to connect them, you realise that you've pushed the wrong button and left them sitting in a telephonic void.

One of the high points of office life is when people photocopy intimate parts of their anatomy and send you the result through the internal mail. The simple answer to this is to sneak in one morning and replace the copier with the shredder. Coffee machines are designed to make people stay at their desks. Whatever button you press you get exactly the same drink: chocolate oxtail coffee.

You won't get promotion by swooning every time your boss makes a little joke and throwing yourself into puddles when they pass; you have to ask. Put your case with a mature, quiet dignity and when they say no follow up with a display of pitiful grovelling in which your pride, dignity and self-respect quickly follow each other out of the window. Round this off by clinging to your boss's leg so that they have to drag you round the office for the rest of the day. If you do get your boss's job you'll find that

you've actually been doing it for the last twenty years while they were 'out with clients'.

When a lift arrives get in. Don't try and hold the door open with any part of your body. Your hand or foot may be successful in keeping the door open but the rest of your body will be twenty floors below. While you're standing in close proximity to a total stranger, acceptable lift conversation should be variations on 'Going up?' It's best to avoid comments like 'Must have a deep shaft.' On visiting small companies don't rush in shouting 'Hold the lift!' Once inside you may find a surprised looking man behind a little desk. He looks surprised because it's not a lift, it's his office.

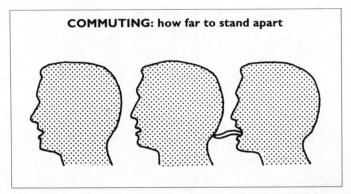

COMMUTING: how far to stand apart

Packed lunch, empty office

As you rise through the office your time is increasingly taken up with lunching and delegating. Delegation is what clears the day for lunch. As you gain experience in industry you will notice that really top people delegate people to delegate for them. You may notice that members of the board seem to develop an ulcerated grouchy look. This is to discourage anyone ever asking *'What exactly is it you do for the company?'*

At your first board meeting you must make every effort not to be impressed by anything. Don't for example say *'this is a nice table.'* Nor should you, if it is a particularly long boardroom table, run up and down it in your socks, skidding right up to the chairman's blotter.

For the board, the only difference between a long lunch and a day off is that you can't claim a day off on expenses. At the end of the meal experienced lunchers slap their Gold Card on the table and say to the waiter *'Try denting that, pal.'*

If you're too busy for a proper lunch, try a strap-on avocado

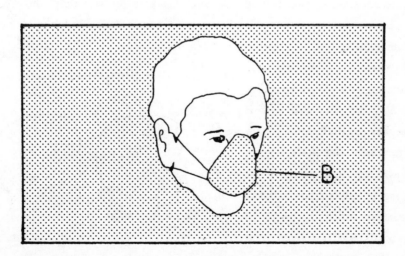

WARNING: *Drinking at lunch is to induce good feelings conducive to client's signatures being put on contracts. It is not to encourage you to stand in the middle of the street with your trousers round your ankles and a traffic cone on your head.*

That's personnel

P ersonnel Departments spend all day sitting round in cosy offices watering potted plants, laughing at how small your salary is and telling you how sad they are that you're leaving. Their other big job is to learn everyone's first name and then trail round the office dropping them as if they were your friend. Always correct them with a new name you've just made up.

The only department that knows more about you than Personnel is the mailroom. This is the friendly place where the kettle is always on, to steam open whatever mail looks exciting. In the mailroom they spend hours practising throwing mail on to desks so that from forty yards they can knock a cup of coffee over a computer keyboard.

ADVICE: *If you're ever confused as to where you stand in the office hierarchy, leaving time will make it clear. You're still a junior if at three seconds past five you tear out of the* building shouting 'FREEDOM!!'. *You're senior if at three seconds past five you return from lunch.*

Top people leave the office at seven, pausing only to patronise the night security staff.

This allows them to return two hours later to do their freelance work, read other people's mail and to transfer the contents of the stationery cupboard into the back of their car.

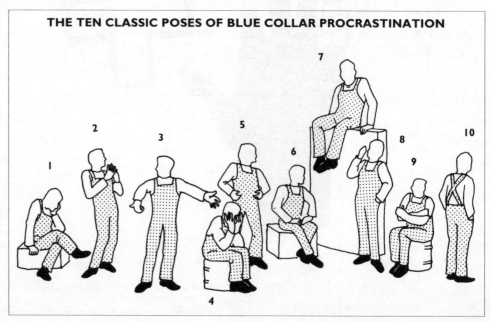

THE TEN CLASSIC POSES OF BLUE COLLAR PROCRASTINATION

14

HEALTH

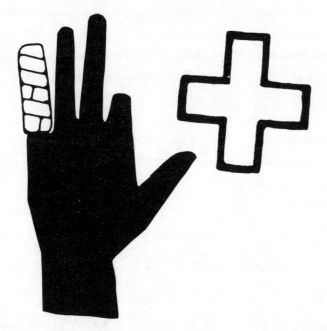

- *I'm fine*

- *Strong as an Ox*

- *Glowing with health*

- *Couldn't be better*

- *Fit as a fiddle*

G enerally, people would be a lot healthier if they weren't ill all the time. The most widespread form of illness is the common cold, and the only known cure for it is the bank holiday.

I'm fine

W hen you go for a check-up, doctors listen to your chest with a stethoscope, hit you on the knee with a small hammer to test your reflexes, and check your blood pressure by inflating a ring around your arm. It's like taking your car for an MOT test and all the mechanic does is put his ear to your bonnet, kick the tyres and put a water wing round the exhaust pipe. In fact, if you examine your bill for £399 closely, that's probably all they have done.

WARNING: *Once in a while doctors like to liven up dull days by insisting that you have an internal examination. This is where you take your trousers down and lie on your side with your bottom poking out. At approximately the same time as the doctor pulls on his rubber glove, a freak breeze blows the net curtains of the surgery aside to reveal a number of interested locals whose wait for the bus has suddenly been much enlivened.*

Doctors' prescriptions are famous for being illegible. That's because they don't want you to read *'give the old trout some coloured aspirin.'* Doctors make furious notes when you describe what's wrong with you, which is all very encouraging until you remember that it's the same writing that he wrote on the last prescription that got you liver salts for a nasty gash on your head. If required, our wonderful doctors will make house calls and you can often see them driving to your house as you are half way to the surgery.

Children have all sorts of special diseases, 90% of which, if mothers are to be believed, make you impotent. Innoculations against whooping cough, German measles and chicken pox are all essential for children. Thankfully these can now all be done with one jab against *Whooping German Pox*. Child-proof tops on bottles of pills mean that 56% of the adult population never get at their prescription, or go mad in the attempt.

If you have an infectious disease, do not expect personal service from your chemist

Strong as an ox

octor's waiting rooms are to the old what nightclubs are to the young; they are where you go to get drugs, discuss the latest movements and pretend there's nothing seriously wrong with you. Waiting rooms generally have two other people in them: one is a very polite man with his severed foot in a Tescos bag; the other is a child whose nose is the world's richest source of mucus. By the time you arrive in the waiting room, the only magazine left is an illustrated catalogue of surgical appliances.

Posters in doctors waiting rooms are specially designed to reduce waiting lists, such as *'Benefits you are entitled to after your death.'* and *'Have you wormed your grandparents?'*

Transplants are a recent advance in medical science that have allowed many livers and kidneys to live long after their owners' death. Of course these transplant miracles would never have happened if it weren't for a great many selfless people who choose to carry around Donor Cards. On these, you can specify which bits you would like to be used to help others to live. It's not therefore a good idea to scrub out all the vital organs and write in *'You can have my willy'*. This is especially so as there is a great deal of evidence to suggest that these organs are often rejected.

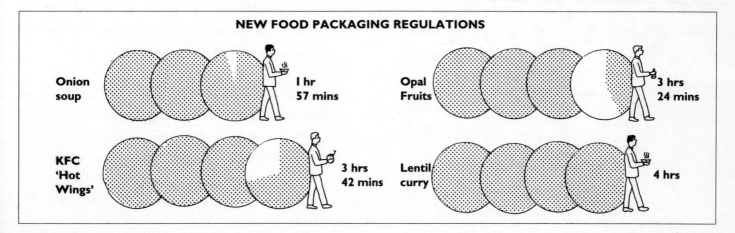

NEW FOOD PACKAGING REGULATIONS

Onion soup — 1 hr 57 mins

KFC 'Hot Wings' — 3 hrs 42 mins

Opal Fruits — 3 hrs 24 mins

Lentil curry — 4 hrs

Glowing with health

O f course, the big thing in health these days is alternative medicine. This holds that for every million pound super drug developed by multi-national drug companies, you can get exactly the same result by pulling something out of your compost and making tea from it. The trouble is, once you know that rhubarb is good for haemorrhoids you can't look a rhubarb crumble in the face again. Acupuncture is a traditional eastern medicine and is good for just about everything except pins and needles. Aromatherapy is the art of using essential oils for healing and relaxation, primrose for constipation, fennel for migraines and Duckhams Hypergrade for all round performance.

OTHER AWFUL THINGS SMOKING IS RESPONSIBLE FOR:	
I	Bad breath
2	The Vietnam War
3	The decline of manufacturing industry
4	The assassination of Martin Luther King
5	Depletion of the ozone, rain forests and whales

Never eat a Vindaloo before a parachute jump

Americans are very hung up about their health, especially on Death Row. There are very many fads in health and many of them start in America. One of these is liposuction, named after the clumsy prom night kiss. Liposuction is where an industrial strength vacuum cleaner is inserted into the patient and surplus fat is sucked out. Environmentally conscious people then recycle this fat and use it to sauté potatoes. Aerobics also came from America. The latest variation on this craze is Agoraphobics, which is exactly the same as aerobics except that you do it in a cupboard.

Couldn't be better

Concern for diet also originated in the states. Health experts generally agree that diet has an important bearing on your general health. What they all agree on is that lack of food can cause death. Apart from that, professional opinion is completely divided. Ask one doctor and she'll tell you that high cholesterol level is the black death of the nineties. Ask another and he'll say *'Don't listen to her, she's fat.'* There are a vast range of diets all specifically designed to make your wallet lighter and your bank balance slimmer. In fact the only diet that has been consistently proven to work is the X-Plan diet; you can eat anything you like, as long as it begins with an 'X'.

In the old days if you needed a tooth out you would go down to the local butchers. If the butcher had a spare moment he would tie a piece of string to your tooth and tie the other end of it to the door. Then he would slam the door. No one can explain why he had to lose his temper at this point. These days the most painful experience you can go through in the dentist's chair is having your wisdom teeth extracted. When a dentist suggests you need to have your wisdom teeth out, always ask for a second opinion. Only go ahead with wisdom teeth extraction if the second opinion recommends castration. If you're given the choice always go for the local anaesthetic, as the last thing you want before the operation is a lot of travelling. Before extraction the dentist will get out a syringe that would make a horse weep.

WARNING: *When the dentist says 'This won't hurt' keep an eye on his nose and see how much it grows.*

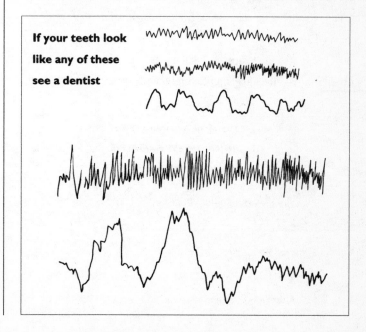

If your teeth look like any of these see a dentist

Fit as a fiddle

Sick office syndrome is where your working environment gives rise to all manner of sore throats and headaches, and obliges you to take time off at home. Medical history only records one case of sick home syndrome, which obliged the sufferer to spend a lot of time at his desk. By law every office has to have one member of staff trained in first aid. In practice, this role is given to the one person who can still dial 999 after a heavy lunch.

Occupational injuries such as tennis elbow and housemaids knee are increasingly widespread. The use of

5 AFFLICTIONS MR TOM WHITEHOUSE, THE UNHEALTHIEST MAN ALIVE, HAS SUFFERED FROM:
I   The Black Death
2   Plague
3   Typhoid
4   Subsidiarity
5   A veritable jet stream of wind

bright red braces in the City during the 1980's gave rise to a high incidence of *'wideboys' nipple'*; *'Parson's nose'* is used to describe a series of nasty rope burns across the face from trying to ring the bell too vigorously after finishing the communion wine; *'Plumber's rash'* are the nasty bedsores workmen get from sleeping through your appointment and seven others they had that day. Fortunately they are insured against this, as any medical treatment required goes on to the bill for fixing your drains.

Hypochondriacs jostle with stamp collecting accountants for the right to be called the dullest people alive. Whatever you're currently afflicted with, they've had it before in a rarer form and developed complications which had doctors puzzled for months. These people come up to you in the office, pull up their shirt and show you an invisible rash on their tummy which they've looked up in a book and are certain is a rare form of eschscholtzia. To shut them up, install a drip feed at your desk that feeds something vital into your arm, and have a little cardiogram that peeps regularly until they start talking to you, and then suddenly stops and won't start again until they've retreated fifty paces.

15

SKIING

- I haven't got the gear

- It's dangerous

- You can get seriously hurt

- People stare at you

- I'd rather stay at home

The British invented skiing, and since then we've been going downhill faster than anyone else. Socially, it's important to know where and when to go. There are certain peak seasons, for example when it's snowing. If, when you're poised at the top of a red run, you find your way blocked by herds of cows being driven up to summer pasture, then you're probably too late. Where you go is equally important. Skiing in Scotland makes as much sense as salmon fishing in the Alps. Look for unspoilt destinations such as Tibet.

I haven't got the gear

It is an unwritten rule that the longer your skis the better skier you are. Aim for ones that are so long that when you are at the top of the slope the tips are already back in the hire shop. Bent poles are also a tell-tale sign of an expert. These can be easily acquired by attempting a black route on your first outing.

WARNING: *When skiing, you will need a lift pass which slides into a special pocket on the outside arm of your ski jacket. Like the filler cap on your car, this is always on the wrong side when you pull up.*

What you wear for skiing is also very important. There's not much point doing a Franz Klammer on the slopes if you do it wearing oilskins and a hand-knitted balaclava. Instead wear a velvet smoking jacket and a pair of plus fours (plus eights if you really want to cut a dash).

If you've got five O levels, you won't need skiing lessons. If you do opt for them, the first thing you learn is the snowplough turn. What happens here is that you find yourself skiing straight into an oncoming snowplough and at the last moment you miraculously discover how to do a turn. Ski instructors speak extremely good English, but tend to favour two words: *'follow'* and *'up-la'*. *'Up-la'*

roughly translates as, *'just do this move that I've been practising every day since I was three'*. Ski instructors may seem romantic but don't be fooled. In reality they are all Reservist Accountants and, should a nasty auditing situation arise, can be behind a desk in a nasty acrylic suit within twenty-four hours.

2 GOLDEN RULES OF SKIING, 1. BEND THE KNEES AND 2. AVOID BUNKERS

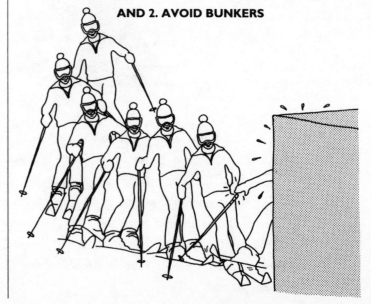

It's dangerous

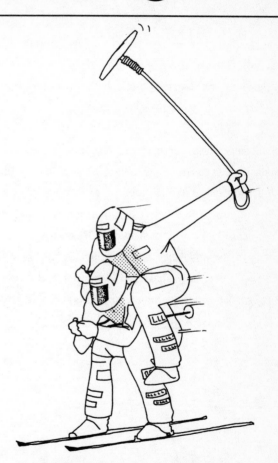

Remember that while skiing is great fun, mountains can be very dangerous places. In seconds you can be caught by a howling blizzard, in blinding snow with temperatures down to minus thirty. So have a couple of barley sugars in your pocket. Unless your name is Torville and Dean stay away from ice. Ski on it and within three seconds you will reach mach 2, and any suggestion of a turn or a braking movement will have both your legs off at the hip. In this situation the only effective method of braking is to ski straight through the thickest part of a beginners ski group.

WARNING: *There are two other causes of death in skiing. One is goggles that mist up in the vicinity of precipices and the other is avalanches. These, like Italians, can be set off with the slightest provocation. In fact a moderately vigorous fart can set half a mountain on the move. So watch your diet.*

The British only excel at an Alpine sport 3 months after they've invented it

WHICH OF THESE COUNTRIES HAS NEVER WON A MEDAL		
IN THE WINTER OLYMPICS?		
1 Austria	4 Lesotho	
2 Norway	5 Canada	
3 France		

Answer : Lesotho

You can get seriously hurt

S kiing, at whatever level, is just about the most dangerous thing you can do on snow, short of streaking at the North Pole. That's why skis now have many clever safety features built into them. For example, if you're involved in a nasty pile up, your skis will immediately fling themselves clear and slip three miles downhill back to the village. This leaves you to walk down in your boots that are so safe you can't bend your ankle in them and you have to walk in a manner that gives rise to a whole rash of yeti sightings. Of course, the worst nightmare for any skier is that they'll break their leg. It's not the pain and the shattered bone that really terrify, it's the thought that someone is going to take a felt tip to your plaster cast and write *'I hope you have it off soon.'*

Button lifts or drag lifts work on the principle that if you're pulled up a mountain by your genitals you're less likely to fall off. Chairlifts would be all right if it weren't for their *'attendants'*. For a start they shepherd you in with the social equivalent of a black hole. Then they helpfully hold the chair back so that instead of slipping comfortably under your bottom, it hits you in the small of the back, flips you over, and drags you upside down half way up the mountain. On the chairlift people always drop things – mittens, poles etc. It makes a terribly good impression if you can drop your underpants. This gives the impression that you got up to something rather bizarre in the chairlift.

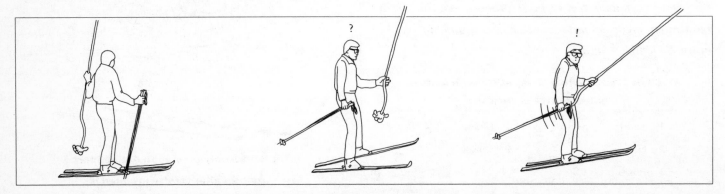

People stare at you

With cable cars there are only two rules. Firstly, unless you want to appear socially challenged, don't try and get in with your skis still on. Secondly, if you're a beginner, don't get in at all. Cable cars do not stop at the top of the nursery slope and your first chance to get out will be at the top of the north face of the Eiger. This is when you realise why no one else has skis on. They're taking the cable car straight back down to the hotel where they will all gather excitedly to watch the tiny figure in a duffel coat attempt a series of controlled snowplough turns down a vertical wall of ice.

To be honest the last thing you want to do when skiing is to ski. Surfboarding is fashionable, but if you really want to make an

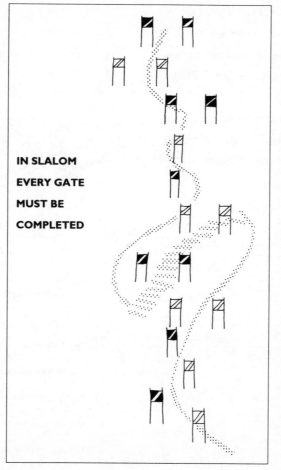

IN SLALOM EVERY GATE MUST BE COMPLETED

impression you should be seen whistling down the black runs on the inflated skin of a water buffalo. If you have to ski, try things like the slalom. This is where you see how quickly you can render yourself impotent by forcing heavy plastic flags between your legs at high speed. There is also a very impressive type of skiing called ski extrème. This involves skiing down slopes that climbers have a tough job getting up. Some of the very hippest continental skiers have taken this even further with ski suicide. This is where you get togged up in your ski kit, you climb in a helicopter, and then hurl yourself out at 10,000 ft. You then do all sorts of fancy hot dogging, parallel turns etc before hitting the tarmac at 240 miles per hour.

105

I'd rather stay at home

F or social climbers the real après-ski starts the minute you get back from your holiday. A week slithering down a slope on your bottom, grabbing on to passing trees, translates as *'yes, we did a lot of fast, off-piste skiing'*. Don't forget, you only have three days to show everybody your tan before you're into the leprosy stage, and chunks of your face start dropping into your coffee. Finally, if skiing really isn't your thing, remember that the ultimate in off-piste skiing is staying at home.

Beware of skiers who have fallen asleep on the slope

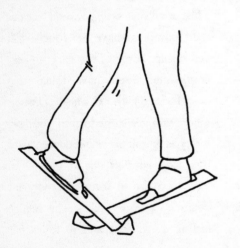

There are few toilet facilities at 10,000 feet

FIVE EVENTS NOT YET INCLUDED IN THE WINTER OLYMPICS
1   The mixed luge
2   The 24 hour gluwein marathon
3   The downhill arse over tit
4   The fifty hoorays in a cable car
5   The stuffing of snow down Susie Dowdall's salopettes

16

ST VALENTINES DAY

☐ *Saint's alive*

☐ *It's me*

☐ *Nothing for you mate*

☐ *Flower Power*

☐ *I'll open it later*

T hose who've experienced both, know that there is little difference between love and indigestion. One way of telling them apart is to remember that indigestion doesn't have a patron saint and there isn't a special day when we can send secret cards to people we know who have indigestion. Love on the other hand has Valentine's Day. This is a special day when people carefully select an expensive card, spend long hours inventing just the right message of love, take every precaution that it is absolutely anonymous and then send it to themselves.

Saint's alive

The tradition of Valentine's Day comes from Valentine, who folded a piece of pink card in half and, in recognition of this miracle, was made a saint. The only other thing we know about Saint Valentine is that he was clubbed to death. There's a moral there somewhere. The fact that Valentine's Day is a fixed point in the calendar means that relationships have to be planned around it.

REMEMBER: *To get any sort of use out of it, you have to be in that* 'undeclared interest' *stage that lasts approximately a day and a half.*

Writing the message inside your card is obviously extremely important. You are unlikely to be original and entertaining if you start with *'roses are red, violets are blue'.*

TEN USEFUL TERMS FOR VALENTINES CARDS:			
1	Ticklepants	6	Floppymoose
2	Snuggledraws	7	Honeytrousers
3	Cuddlepumpkin	8	Tangobotty
4	Tinklefritter	9	Wonderdumpling
5	Sugarpetal	10	Duvetbuggy

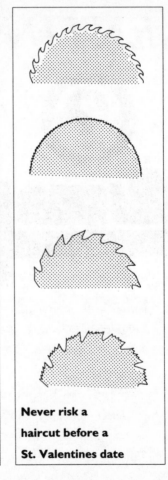

Never risk a haircut before a St. Valentines date

After three hours soul searching and bloodletting all you are likely to produce is *'roses are red, violets are blue, bananas are yellow, you're a hell of a fellow.'* Try and avoid reworking the classics. There's no point calling in Shakespeare's help if you're then going to come up with, *'Shall I compare thee to a Cheeseburger.'* Once you've settled on the message, the next step is to disguise your handwriting. A tried and tested way is to clench a golf ball in your hand and then pummel your fist into a bucket full of gravel until you have lost all feeling and sensitivity in it on a permanent basis. Then type your message.

It's me

One of the great problems on Valentine's Day is how to send an anonymous card but at the same time make damn sure that the recipient can work out who it's from.

USEFUL TIP: *If you live in Zambia and you're posting the card to London then the brightly coloured stamp with the parrot may act as a subtle hint.*

If, on the other hand, you're posting anything in Britain, don't rely on the postmark. If you do, your letter will inevitably pass through the hands of *'Smudger'* Latham, renowned for his sloppy franking.

To be absolutely sure they know who you are, you should accidentally glue your business card to the envelope, add *'if undelivered please return to'* to the back of the envelope and enclose a stamped addressed envelope.

If you have any doubts, heavily disguise your voice, and make a guarded phone call, saying something along the lines of *'have you got my card yet?.'*

One tricky problem is when some utterly repellent 'human' being approaches you and says *'you sent me this card didn't you'*. The only possible answer is *'yes I did, but it was for a dare!'*

RHINO HORN IS A POWERFUL APHRODISIAC

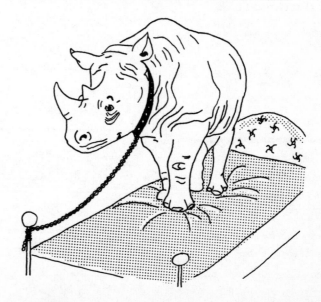

Nothing for you Mate

However hard you struggle against it, it is impossible to receive nothing on Valentine's Day and not feel like the leper from the void. That's why when the only item of post is some junk mail from the local pet shop, you can convince yourself that it is in fact an incredibly well disguised Valentine, and that if only you could decipher it, *'Free sack of aquarium gravel'* must surely be an anagram for *'You are my sweetest valentine.'*

WARNING: *As part of its new Customer First policy the post office are now introducing a stop-me-and-buy-one service where the postman will sell you a card and sign it on your door step. The following day he will then deliver the first of many blackmail notes.*

FIVE THINGS MORE IMPORTANT THAN RECEIVING A VALENTINE'S CARD

1 The elimination of hunger throughout the world

2 An end to war wherever it is happening

3 Harmony between countries, creeds and colours

4 A new spirit of co-operation and mutual respect between the sexes based on an understanding of their differences and a joint celebration of what they both hold in common

5 Receiving a card from the person you were hoping to receive it from

---

BETWEEN 6 AM – 8AM ON ST VALENTINE'S DAY

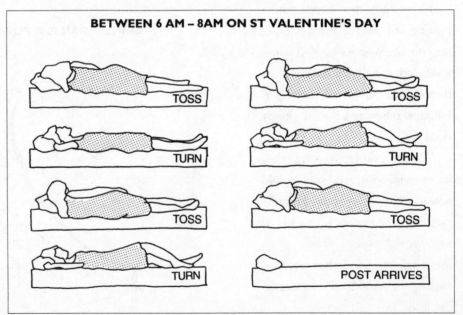

TOSS
TOSS
TURN
TURN
TOSS
TOSS
TURN
POST ARRIVES

Flower Power

I f you want something to arrive on the 14th don't rely on the post office. The 24p you pay for a first class stamp includes 18p for transportation and 6p for storage. Many people now deliver their message of love through various forms of singing telegram. Beware of the Inland Revenue-o-gram. This is where a team of tax inspectors calls on you with all your old tax returns, you're dragged off to court, convicted of seven counts of tax evasion and spend three years in an open prison. Two years into your sentence you realise that the Inland Revenue-o-gram was none other than the Inland Revenue and the fact that you laughed hysterically throughout your trial probably didn't do you any favours at all.

Another marvellous Valentine's Day tradition is declaring your love through an announcement in the paper. These are heavily disguised and are characterised by their witty terms of endearments, such as *'Pram for sale. One dodgy wheel. £25.'* To make a really big impression you have to do something a little special. Hiring a small plane and skywriting the name of your loved one is a good idea.

WARNING: *don't attempt this if you have a Polish girlfriend called Plyzinch Ctzyclyviwa as you're very likely to stall into a fatal tailspin between the z and the y. Again, think twice about this if your beloved lives in the Gatwick area.*

In micro-biological terms there is not a great deal of difference between a bunch of roses and a sack of turnips. Take this as a warning if you're expecting anything from a micro-biologist. If you're trying to say it with flowers, sending a plastic tulip is the equivalent of a speech impediment. Sending red roses is a succinct way of saying, *'I've got the imagination of a peanut'.* Remember, giving flowers has nothing to do with delicate little posies of hand-picked wild flowers; it has everything to do with vast windows of crackling cellophane and the powerful fragrance of credit cards.

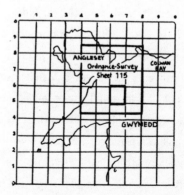

Most probable location of women called 'Gwynedd'

I'll open it later

R eceiving a Valentine's card in the office can put you in a nasty spot. Business correspondence never, ever comes in pink envelopes that smell like a tart's hanky. There's no point therefore in putting it in your in-tray and pretending to deal with it along with all the other mail.

REMEMBER: *Whatever time of the day you choose to open it, you can bet that a party of eighteen work mates will accidentally coalesce round your desk seconds after you slip your finger under that little pink fold. They will shortly be joined by the office swat who has collected samples of everybody's handwriting in the office for you to compare against.*

Once you've opened it, never let anyone have a look. Even if you show it only to your two closest colleagues, it will inevitably find its way into a photocopier, the company newsletter and the annual report.

If you are fortunate enough to get a Valentine, never throw it away. Send it to yourself Datapost and you will receive it the following year. If at the end of the 14th you've spent hundreds on postage, herniated your brain trying to dream up clever little messages, done a series of life endangering stunts, and your beloved is still as responsive as a bollard, don't worry. There are plenty more fish in the sea; if you're ready to go out with a fish, that is.

THE ESSENCE OF ROMANCE IS SUBTLEY

CONVERSATION

C onversation is the essential lubricant of social intercourse. Boons as they are in mining disasters, strong silent types are at less of a premium on the cocktail circuit.

Getting started

F irst words in company are listened to as critically as the first words of babies. The rate of your social ascent will be determined by your choice between *'hallo'*, *'hello'* and *'hullo'*. The later the operative vowel comes in the alphabet the greater the social impact. Social progress will be abruptly terminated if you say *'hillo.'*

Steer clear of any greetings you couldn't imagine the Queen Mother using, including monosyllables such as *'Hi'*, *'Yo'*, *'Oi'* and anything that resembles a grunt. Make sure extra syllables don't creep into otherwise acceptable greetings. Note the difference between *'How do you do?'* and *'How do you do it?'*.

An opening conversational gambit that crops up with

FIVE EXCEEDINGLY BAD WAYS TO START A CONVERSATION WITH A MAN IF YOU'RE A WOMAN

1 *'Hello, I'm married'*

2 *'You remind me of my goofy kid brother'*

3 *'To me penis size is the main thing'*

4 *'You better keep those elbows in, fatboy'*

5 *'All men are rapists'*

---

monotonous regularity is *'so what line are you in?'* Replying *'I'm in the line for the toilet.'* usually stops that one dead. If they persist in enquiring, tell them that you drive a TV licence detector van, and then shortly afterwards ask them where they live. There is one opening gambit that it's best to avoid completely as you will never recover from it; *'I hope you're good at conversation because I'm hopeless.'*

One of the hazards of conversation is having to look at people at close range. Few faces are perfect and there is usually something to distract you such as nose hair long enough for bungee jumping. If you notice that the top of the Copydex is stuck to someone's hairpiece on no account mention it. Simply natter away in a breezy fashion and wrestle with the offending item as if you were chatting to someone while pruning.

Standing opposite someone, you are also bound to notice what they're wearing. Clothing is a touchy subject so avoid remarks such as *'Did you get dressed in the dark?'* Any comments at all should be addressed in a neutral speak-your-weight kind of voice, *'That's certainly some clothing you've got on there.'* However don't let neutrality become stupidity, *'Is that clothing you're wearing?'*

Duck-billed platitudes

Discussions on topics of which you know nothing can be indefinitely prolonged with the repeated use of, *'There's a lot of truth in that'* and *'we've all been there'*. If you are suddenly asked something and you don't understand the question let alone the answer simply say, *'Before I answer that, I must ask you whether anyone has ever commented on your resemblance to Arnold Schwarznegger?'* (Use this one sparingly with women.)

Questions like, *'What do you mean by that?'* are always good for helping things along, but be careful. Harmless though it may seem, this question repeated several times in succession begins to probe the metaphysical underpinning of a person's existence and if you don't watch out you can end up with a suicide on your hands.

Conversation and intelligence don't readily mix. That's why academics are rarely worth talking to because more often than not they're worried that if they make the effort to remember who you are, they'll forget the name of a rare fish. In general, there's nothing that stops a good old natter faster than somebody trying to be clever. For example if you were trying to pass the time of day with T. S. Eliot, you wouldn't get past telling him you'd just been to the shops before he chimed in with *'We must not cease from exploration. And the end of all our exploring will be to arrive where we began and to know the place for the first time.'* The only response to that or any other nonsense is, *'Nice cup of tea?'*

TALKING TO COMPUTER BUFFS CAN BE A MONUMENTAL DRAG

```
330 IF KS=CHRS(133) THEN S=S1
340 IF KS=CHRS(134) THEN S=S2
350 IF KS=CHRS(135) THEN S=S3
360 IF KS=CHRS(136) THEN S=NOISE
400 REM play a note
410 IF KS="Q" THEN POKE S,189
420 IF KS="W" THEN POKE S,197
430 IF KS="E" THEN POKE S,203
440 IF KS="R" THEN POKE S,206
450 IF KS="T" THEN POKE S,214
```

Talk amongst yourself

During dinner party conversations it may happen that both your neighbours are having riveting conversations with the person on their other side and the person opposite is cut off by a dense flower arrangement.

WARNING: *This conversational limbo feels great for approximately thirty seconds, and then you rapidly feel like an oversized prune.*

PSYCHOLOGICAL TRACKING OF WEAK JOKE

effort   overcompensation   recovery   exhaustion

FIVE EXCEEDINGLY BAD WAYS TO START A CONVERSATION WITH A WOMAN IF YOU'RE A MAN
1 *'I was hoping to sit next to someone younger'*
2 *'Do you cut your own hair?'*
3 *'My grandmother's got a dress just like that'*
4 *'Shouldn't you consider dieting or something?'*
5 *'It's amazing how many wrinkles you've packed onto your neck'*

You can try looking across to the far side of the table and pretending you're listening with interest to a distant conversation, but be careful that all this staring blankly into the distance doesn't begin to resemble madness on your part.

If you've been left in complete silence for an hour or more rap on your glass with a spoon. This is guaranteed to get everyone's attention. However, you may find it tricky knowing what to do next so have a witty and entertaining speech prepared.

Quick to the cut

Cutting people dead is one of the great bloodsports of the social scene. Just before someone's punch line touch them lightly (not the groin), say *'would you excuse me?'* and walk purposefully off as if something terribly important needs your immediate attention. Complete the effect by stopping five feet away for some trifling banter with someone of limited social consequence.

On the other hand it can be most annoying when you're making a big effort to slime up to someone and they keep looking at other people over your shoulder. Wait until they're having a long stare at the group behind you then quickly duck away, circle round and join it. This shows that not only are you with the group they're so interested in, but also that they're now talking to themselves.

Every person you talk to has a topic that you simply shouldn't mention, generally death, divorce or hair loss, or, if you're really unlucky, all three. Sometimes, just when you think you've kindled a decent conversation, you say something on the face of it perfectly innocuous, and the person you've spoken to bursts into tears. Whatever you said the damage has been done so don't back-pedal.

USEFUL TIP: *If they're crying, cry louder. Tear at your clothes, writhe around on the floor and then beat your head against a wall until it's caked with blood. After half an hour of this your initial blunder will have been forgotten. If it hasn't, apologise.*

HOW TO SPEAK PITMAN'S SHORTHAND

Friendship...   **is a treasured...**   **possesion...**

Wild bores

In a party situation never get caught by yourself in the open. Within seconds a dull person can pin you down and administer the conversational equivalent of a general anaesthetic. You can never be too careful. Dull people sometimes dress up as interesting people and fool everybody until they say, *'Hillo, have you ever really thought about sandpaper.'* Also, beware of potted plants. Dull people hide behind them and spring out as you pass on your way to the loo.

Anecdotes are conversation cloggers of the worst sort. If someone says *'have I told you about..?'* answer *'yes'* even if it's the first time you've met. Once an anecdote is under way, derail it by saying *'Is this the one where the*

Videophones will spell the end of teledating

AA man jump-starts her kidney machine?' It won't be and nor will it be anywhere near as interesting.

As a social climber you must check regularly that your conversation is having the desired effect. Positive signs to watch for are people you're talking to clapping, writing you cheques and taking off their clothes. Danger signs include the lights going out, the doors being locked and you being the last person in the room. If you find that your attempts at conversation are almost invariably accompanied by one or all of these danger signs, then you must learn to wear clothes that make a statement so deafening that any form of verbal communication is unnecessary.

THE CORRECT RESPONSE TO ANECDOTES

18

CULTURE

- *Ballet poor show*
- *Art is hell*
- *Small screen, small talk*
- *Reading gaol*
- *Proper Opera*

C rude oiliness will only get you so far in the social world. Refinement is also needed and this means knowing what book the bookies back for the Booker, what the difference is between Manet and Man U, and what relation William Turner is to Tina Turner.

Ballet poor show

When you arrive in the foyer keep an eye out for the giant with the afro and running sore on the back of his neck. You'll be seeing him later; he'll be sitting in front of you.

Ballet is based on a fundamental misunderstanding of human nature. A man sees a woman he fancies, he prances towards her with his hands above his head and then stands on tip toe. Then, once they get to know each other, the man takes the woman and holds her above his head with her skirt in his face.

FIVE PLACES WHERE YOUR CHANCES OF ENCOUNTERING CULTURE ARE SLIM:

1   The Wolverhampton Grand

2   The Bolton Alhambra

3   The Romford Empire

4   The Port Talbot Roxy

5   Canada

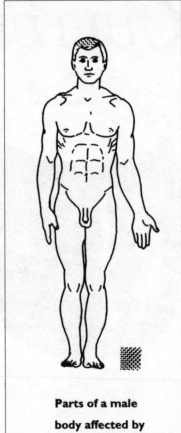

Parts of a male body affected by high culture

REMEMBER: *This doesn't work in real relationships and may explain why so many ballet stars have such miserable love lives.*

First time ballet goers often wonder how the men sweep the women into the air so easily. The trick to this manoeuvre is a special step built into the front of the man's tights. The ballerina leaps up on to the step and pushes off from it.

NOTE: *After this particular move you'll notice that for the rest of the act the man doesn't move around much.*

Art is hell

Y ou can spot an American in an art gallery a mile off. They come in, see a painting and say *'Will you look at that'* and then they do. The British would rather take a close look at the tea room or gift shop. But you can only stay there for so long. Sooner or later you have to look at a painting and make an aesthetic judgement. Reading the little descriptive plaque won't help. All they say is: *'Saved for the Nation by Hitachi.'* At some stage you have to stand in front of a painting and look at it. Remember at this time what Schopenhauer said; *'We should comport ourselves with the masterpieces of art as with exalted personages – stand quietly before them until they speak to us.'* Remember too, that Schopenhauer wore flares and had no friends.

DON'T FORGET: *Whenever you're talking about modern art, bear in mind that you're perfectly entitled to think* 'What a load of rubbish' *as long as what you actually say is* 'This is a masterful articulation of the form-content dialectic, delicately cantilevered on internal tensions.'

Modern Art, like junk bonds, is for speculative purposes only. Bear this in mind when you're asked to comment on a piece in someone's home. Say *'That must be worth a very great deal.'* If it is, you're laughing and if it isn't they're going to start wondering why they've hung up something that looks like a towel in an Intercity toilet. Always remember that the art world has no sense of humour. That's why you don't see car stickers saying *'Royal Academicians are well hung.'*

THE BASIC PHYSICAL PRINCIPLE UNDERLYING ALL HIGHER FORMS OF ART

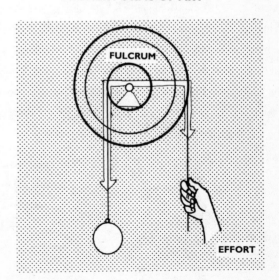

Small screen, small talk

W atching television isn't much use if you're hoping to make an impression in society; unless of course you're watching in bed with a minor Royal. In conversation, try asking if somebody saw that delightful little programme on Etruscan pottery the other night. If they didn't, say *'shame'* in a way that implies that they were watching the darts on ITV. If, by a miracle, they did, say *'Shame. You missed the darts.'*

Chat shows are to the media world what colonic irrigation is to the medical world. Chat shows are a chance for various celebrities to talk in an informal way about their new book, to be asked searching, probing questions about their new book and to tell some amusing anecdotes about their new book. If there's time at the end they may also mention their new book. But first here's a song called *'Have you heard about his new book?'*

The reputation of Chinese acrobats rests heavily on their starched shirts

Computers are rapidly catching up with human intelligence

USEFUL TIP: *Most televisions now have a remote control, which means you can switch between the channels and watch several programmes at once.*

This does have its advantages. Let's say you'd been zapping between Minder, The Business Programme and Blockbusters. The following day, if you were stopped in the street by a researcher who asked you what you'd watched the night before, you could reply quite truthfully, 'Mind your own business, buster.'

Reading gaol

*I*n society, the only book you have to worry about is Debrett's, which lists the country's nobs. It's not a difficult book to get in. Simply come across with William the Conqueror, shove the Anglo-Saxons off their land and then sit tight for the next nine hundred years, quietly cultivating a recessed chin and a braying voice.

For your coffee table don't bother with huge glossy hardbacks such as the AA Book of Droppings. It's your bookmarks you'll be judged on. If you're on chapter two of A Brief History of Time don't mark your achievement with a frilly bookmark from Torquay. Arty postcards from Berlin are good, shopping lists with improbable items from Fortnums are excellent, or go for gold with a battered invitation to a Royal garden party with *'must try and fob her off'* scribbled on it.

Never get caught reading Readers' Digest. You won't get very far if people think you're secretly enriching your word power.

Classical concerts will test even the hardiest socialite. Try to avoid involuntary stabbing at a non-existent fast-forward button. Experienced concert-goers look suitably rapt by assuming the sort of stunned, glazed look you get when someone has just bounced a basketball in your face.

At some stage you may find that after you've clapped, walked half way up the aisle and said in a loud voice, *'Where did you leave the car, Terry?'* the orchestra starts up again. This is because you've just had a short break between movements. The appropriate behaviour during these breaks is to cough. The better the performance the louder the cough. If you really want to impress, see if you can't cough up some blood.

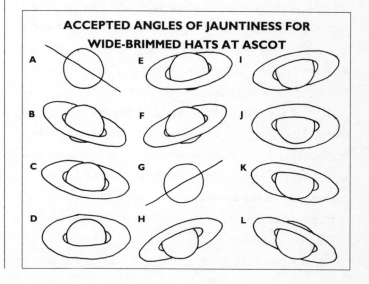

ACCEPTED ANGLES OF JAUNTINESS FOR WIDE-BRIMMED HATS AT ASCOT

Proper Opera

To enjoy opera you will need a pillow, blanket, eye mask, Walkman and a selection of your favourite tapes. Don't forget the hacksaw to saw off your legs in the interval, as by that stage you will have lost the use of them anyway. That's why people always spring up at the end of an opera. What sounds like *'Bravo!'* and *'Encore!'* is actually *'God my leg, it's completely dead!'*

WARNING: *On the seat in front of you there is a little pair of plastic opera glasses. These glasses have a special lens that makes the stage seem smaller and puts someone's head in the middle of it. Opera novices spend most of the first act flicking them on and off their face to see if they make the slightest difference. They don't, and that's why nobody has stolen a pair for over a century.*

Bars at interval time are like the Harrods sale, except that in Harrods you eventually get served. You can forget drinks altogether if you have the sort of bar presence that says *'Don't worry, I enjoy waiting.'* Instead go to the nearest tray of pre-bought drinks, scribble the word Rev. in front of the name and start to drink in a pious way.

The key word in opera is *'libretto'*. In the interval say, *'What a marvellous libretto.'* Or, if it's an Italian opera, *'What a marvellous lambretta.'* And remember, it's not over until the fat lady finishes her Maltesers.

There are two types of seats in major theatres, the good ones at the front which let you watch the stars spray each other with spittle, and the bad ones at the back which are so steeply raked that you have to wear a harness to prevent you plummeting into the orchestra pit.

Of course the place to aim for is a private box. The point of these is not that you get a good view of the stage, but rather that the audience get a good view of you. Once they're all looking, set up your portable television set and watch EastEnders.

FIVE FRINGE SHOWS THAT NEVER MADE THE WEST END

1. Cheltenham Ladies Amateur Dramatics Society production of *'Gazza; World Cup Magic'*

2. My Ego Revisited by the Oxbridge Theatre Company

3. Terminator 2 on ice

4. Pirates of Penzance by the Wormwood Scrubs Drama Group

5. Miserable Cat on Phantom Express: The compilation show

19

RESTAURANT

- Indian reservation

- Cachet check

- In the soup

- Table talk

- Is this bill upside down?

W hen you're out for the night, you should look on the restaurant as the base camp from which the summit of the bedroom can be attempted. You won't go far wrong if you obey the two golden rules: Don't eat with your mouth full, and don't speak with your mouth open.

Indian reservation

G oing for an Indian won't get you very far socially. There is something about a curry that is deflationary to social pretensions. Choose a Cambodian or Vietnamese restaurant on the basis that social desirability of oriental cuisines increases with CIA involvement in their country of origin. However chic sushi may sound, remember that eating it is like having your nose run directly into your mouth. Steer clear of oriental food altogether if you're still at the stage where you hold a chopstick in each hand. Continental food should be from south Europe only; no one has ever made significant social progress by ordering Weinerschnitzel.

FIVE THINGS YOU SHOULDN'T EXPECT TO FIND IN HIGH CLASS RESTAURANTS:
1 C2/ D2s
2 Large bottles of vinegar
3 Old people nursing a cup of tea over three of four hours
4 Leaflets explaining how nutritious their food is contrary to press reports
5 An Irish Wolfhound waiting patiently at your table and looking at every mouthful with a wistful longing look.

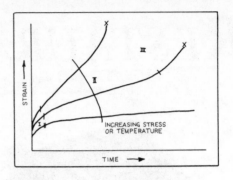

Don't expect to get a table just because you rang earlier. Between phoning and arriving anything can happen. A bad restaurant can be under new management and a good restaurant can get a call *'Table for twenty-four, name of Windsor'*.

If when you ring the manager says, *'Thank God you phoned, come when you like, and bring as many people as possible'*, cancel.

Sign legally required to be displayed on the back of Tandoori menus

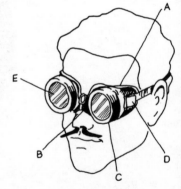

In Chinese restaurants it is essential to be protected against sizzling dishes

Cachet check

When you first sit down there is an uneasy moment of intimacy when you are suddenly face to face, with no menus to hide behind. Resist the urge to look away. You will only see your sheepish face reflected in a mirror whose irregularities give the impression that the elephant man is sitting at the next table.

On the other hand, a glance in the mirror may give you last minute warning of that leaf of cabbage that has found its way between your two front teeth, despite you not having touched cabbage since primary school.

Occupy yourself by checking the crockery. If you suspect that the crockery is plastic, pick up your plate and give it a sharp rap on the edge of the table. If it bounces back and dents your forehead you were right to be suspicious. If on the other hand it shatters then it's fine bone China, you're in a good restaurant and you can relax.

No one impresses by the size of their tooth pick

Flamboyancy in chefs can be counterproductive

They're called waiters because you have to wait. Most waiters are unemployed actors except the one that takes your order. Between taking your order and bringing you your food he has to slip out to play Henry IV Parts I and 2.

There are two ways to attract waiters' attention. The easiest way is to grow up with the waiter, become his closest friend and, having saved his life, get him to promise that if he ever becomes a waiter he'll hear your surreptitious coughs. If this fails, grab a loose piece of their clothing and yank them towards you. They love this.

On arrival the waiter will run through the *'special'* at three hundred words a minute. Don't bother getting them to repeat it, just say *'What's special about that?'*

In the soup

I f you're ever served a whole crab in a restaurant you may think you're facing the ultimate test in decorum. The truth is you can do anything you like with the crab because everyone forms their opinion of your eating manners on how you tackle the simplest of things, the soup.

At home most of us favour the traditional air-sea rescue method; this is where you hover as low as possible over the bowl and scoop it safely aboard. In restaurants, it's a different story. You must sit ramrod straight and lift a spoon brimful of soup through a vast distance up to your mouth. It only takes the slightest lapse of concentration for your soup to find its way back to the bowl with a thin piddling sound.

The tricky business of finishing your soup starts when, had you been at home, the Peter Rabbit motif would be surfacing through the soup. Don't scrape at the bowl and do little Moses manoeuvres, parting the soup down the middle. Tip the bowl away from you and dip the spoon in and up as if you were in fact trying to feed the person opposite you. The first two or three times you attempt this your soup will shoot over the lip of the bowl onto the white linen tablecloth. However, you will be remembered for your good

intentions rather than for your lack of co-ordination. '*Remembered*' because of course you won't be eating with that person again.

One warning about soup. If it's hot and liquid and comes in a bowl it's a pretty safe bet it's soup, but it might be a finger bowl. If you've politely swallowed the contents of the finger bowl, you can carry the whole thing off by washing your fingers in the soup.

Table talk

*T*he amount you eat is in inverse proportion to the amount you talk. If you allow yourself a sustained conversational flourish, be prepared to get a plateful of cold Brussel sprouts down in under thirty seconds whilst being stared at by the rest of the restaurant who are all wondering why the noise has stopped.

REMEMBER: *If you decide to eat before talking don't forget to leave a couple of mouthfuls on the plate in case you drop an absolute clanger and suddenly feel a desperate need to busy yourself with your food again. When your own conversation starts to flag, it's worth tuning in to the next table. The risk here is that they may be having an animated discussion on what a dreadful person you are.*

At really swank restaurants there will be large serviettes and at least two fine linen tablecloths. That's a lot of material to deal with and it may happen that you accidentally tuck the tablecloth into your trousers.

If then you get up to go to the loo you may find you pull the whole tablecloth off and drag it and thousands of pounds worth of crockery and glassware across the floor. Don't call attention to yourself by over reacting. Simply say *'excuse me'*, dab at your mouth with the offending end of the table cloth, and quietly settle in Peru.

In any romantic candle-lit dinner for two, there are two key moments to watch for: one is when you're asked if you're free to join the other person on their yacht in Antigua – and the other is when you discover you have a mouthful of gristle that a shark couldn't swallow. Generally these two moments coincide.

A practice increasingly common in restaurants is to give you a hot towel when you have finished your meal. It is quite proper to wash your face with this cloth and, if it is convenient, you should also have a quick stab at your armpits, especially if you think someone might be getting close to them later in the evening. When you have finished with them, the waiter will take your towels back to the kitchens to be boiled up for tomorrow's soup.

THE SIX LEAST POPULAR NAMES FOR RESTAURANTS:			
1	The Slops Bucket	4	The Curry Botty
2	The Cockroach	5	Le Gastro Enteritis
3	El Salmonella	6	Station Buffet

Is this bill upside down?

I f you want the bill don't put up your hand and make little ticking manoeuvres. Waiters have no idea what this means and you can end up being brought anything from rubber gloves to sewing kits. To make yourself understood, do a realistic mime of getting the bill, complete with staring eyes, choking, calculators and tense meetings with accountants. Waiters very often bring a mint with the bill. This is a shrewd psychological move to freshen your mouth up after the appaling meal you have just eaten, and to put you in a better frame of mind for the tipping.

ADVICE: *Tipping varies between 15% and 20%. The other 80% don't bother.*

Judge whether conditions are right for an assault on the bedroom by the final drinks ordered. If your partner orders a hot chocolate for a good night's sleep there's no use in you then having a triple espresso for all-night alertness and fifteen After Eights for extra energy. If you've failed on this score, the taxi ride back must be devoted to convincing them that you enjoyed the evening a lot less than they did, and that in fact you're going on to somewhere a lot more interesting.

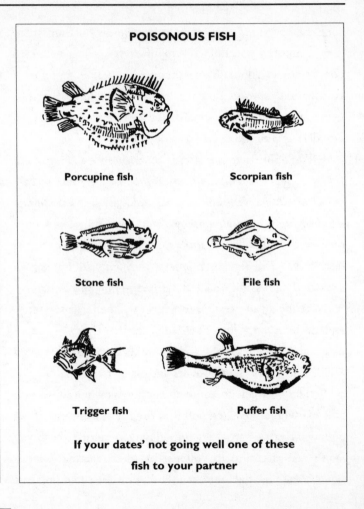

POISONOUS FISH

Porcupine fish

Scorpian fish

Stone fish

File fish

Trigger fish

Puffer fish

If your dates' not going well one of these fish to your partner

20

CHRISTMAS

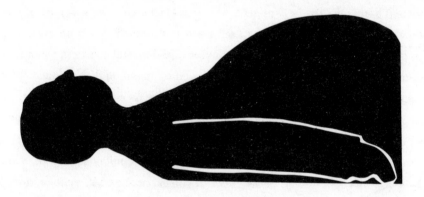

- [ ] *Let us pay*

- [ ] *Give us this day*

- [ ] *It is more blessed to give*

- [ ] *Deck the halls*

- [ ] *Ding dong merrily*

C hristmas, like the sperm whale, comes but once a year. For Christmas shoppers and sperm whales alike, its best to start thinking about it a long way in advance. You'll know when Christmas is approaching when credit card companies send in snatch squads to repossess your wallet, when pear trees are packed with partridges and when you finally finish the bottle of '*Messerschmitt*' aftershave you got last year.

Let us pay

The good thing about Christmas shopping is that it prepares you for the January sales. Christmas shopping is like American Football without the helmets; there's a lot of grunting and crashing and when you look up you've moved one yard, you've got three teeth missing and someone's bought your trousers. There are two basic rules to remember when Christmas shopping: Firstly, you've done enough when you start trying to buy things on your kidney donor card; secondly, when buying presents, bear in mind that it's the thought that counts but the receipt that matters. Before you send Christmas cards its best to prepare a list. Write down all your friends' names, cross out all those who you secretly dislike, go out and buy two cards.

Christmas Eve is a magical and mysterious time and one of the biggest mysteries is why half the furniture in the house disappears before midnight. The answer to this riddle appears round the Christmas tree the following

6 hours of continuous wrapping can transform a modestly priced biro into a substantial offering

morning, when there are some familiar looking objects such as kettles and ironing boards covered in wrapping paper. Traditionally children whine a lot on Christmas Eve in a concerted effort to be allowed to open one present before Christmas Day. Tell them they can open one small, cheap present. This will keep them happy as long as you remember not to tell them that one small, cheap present is all they're getting this year. Children still believe in Santa Claus up to the age of three months or so, and therefore Christmas Eve is when you have to sneak into their bedroom and fill their stockings. Unfortunately if you go in anytime before five o'clock in the morning, your little treasure will whisper, *'Daddy, if you don't stop coming in and out, Santa Claus will never come.'* If you get tired of this, try some ether.

FOUR PEOPLE WHO HAVE TO WORK THROUGH CHRISTMAS:
1 The two pages who hold the Queen's corgis during Her Majesty's address to the Commonwealth
2 The man with his finger on the trigger of Britain's nuclear deterrent
3 The man who makes the strong coffee for the man with his finger on the trigger of Britain's nuclear deterrent
4 The woman in Bournemouth who is trying to beat the world endurance record for continuous whingeing

Give us this day

S ome people are so damned thoughtful that if you make some passing comment in April about how useful non-stick frying pans are, you'll end up with seven round the tree. For the next twenty years whenever your name and Christmas are mentioned in the same breath the conversation will include *'he does like non-stick frying pans you know.'* Without question the most irritating present to receive is anything that is handmade. The worst things about these lovingly knitted medieval jockstraps is that there's no way you can take them back. You can try unravelling them and taking the wool back to the shop, but it's a bit of a last resort.

There are three phrases traditionally used during unwrapping. *'What lovely paper, its a shame to spoil it'*, *'It's a lovely little guards van, but I sold my train set thirty years ago, gran,'* and *'I wonder what this frying pan shaped object is.'* Every Christmas includes a present that makes you smart with disappointment. This is generally from the one you love and is evidence that they won't take even the broadest hint however often and from whatever height it is dropped. Everyone has a relative abroad at Christmas, so as soon as you see a bitterly disappointing present emerging

from the wrapping, distract attention by jumping up and shouting *'We must phone Fritz!!'*

REMEMBER: *Thank you notes should be sent to arrive three hours before the shops close on Christmas Eve and should read, 'Thank you for your enormously expensive and thoughtful gift.'*

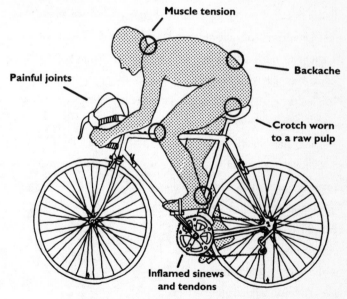

Muscle tension

Painful joints

Backache

Crotch worn to a raw pulp

Inflamed sinews and tendons

Five powerful reasons for not getting over excited when you get a bike for Xmas

133

It is more blessed to give

Christmas hampers sound like the small irritating people that get in your way during last minute shopping. They are in fact laundry baskets packed with spam that people give to each other at Christmas to subtly imply *'you don't eat very well normally.'* Gift vouchers are also an excellent idea. A £5 pet shop token means to all intents and purposes you have given a tub of maggots. Vast quantities of alcohol are bought at Christmas mostly in the form of aftershave. If you have to buy perfume don't ever get the original. For half the price of Chanel No. 5 you can pick up some convincing smelling *'Chanel Tunel'*.

Some people choose to dilute the essentially commercial nature of Christmas by going to church. This can be hazardous. Regulars deliberately try and give the johnny-come-latelys a hard time by throwing in a raft of

Charades :

'Ben Hur' in four easy steps.

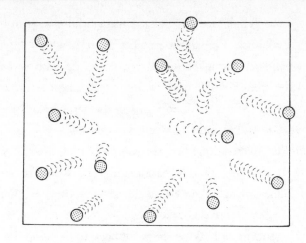

Aerial view of clinically anti-social people at christmas party

extra kneeling-downs, standing-ups and gratuitous crossings so that the service becomes an extended aerobics session. Carol singing is an excuse for the Neighbourhood Watch to go round in packs, stand outside *'offenders'* houses and shout their heads off. In Scotland an important part of the festive season is *'first footing'*. This is an old Highland tradition of pretending you're tall dark and handsome, throwing coal through your neighbour's window and then hot footing it back to your croft.

Deck the halls

Many so-called Christmas traditions, like stuffing Christmas puddings full of silver sixpences, are complete myths. If you adjust for inflation the average Victorian would have been burying the equivalent of five years' wages in his Christmas pudding. A more recent tradition is setting fire to the Christmas pudding. This generally happens half way through cooking it.

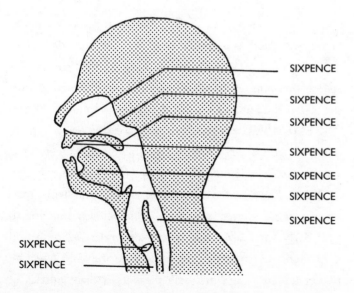

SIXPENCE
SIXPENCE
SIXPENCE
SIXPENCE
SIXPENCE
SIXPENCE
SIXPENCE
SIXPENCE
SIXPENCE

X - ray 2 hours after eating traditional Christmas pudding.

Technological advances have rendered some traditional customs obsolete. For example, modern materials such as lycra mean that Christmas stockings that used to have a job accommodating a satsuma, can now swallow a couple of watermelons with ease. Advent calendars now come in special double glazed versions where you have a hell of a job getting any of the windows open. Christmas crackers of old used to have jokes such as, *'What's green and sings? Elvis Parsley!!'* and small plastic cowboys. Modern taste in humour has moved on considerably, which is why crackers now have jokes such as *'What's green and sings? Elvis Parsley!!'* and small plastic cowboys.

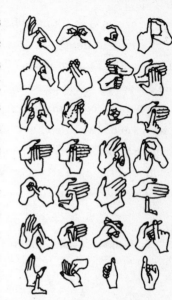

Rabbit silhouettes aren't as easy as they appear.

Ding dong merrily

Christmas is a time when relatives emerge who cast serious doubt on Darwin's theories of evolution. These are the sort of relatives who put on their paper hats and suddenly look more sophisticated. No Christmas is complete without the niece who overdoses on brandy butter and rides her new bicycle over her brother's spanking new hamster. Another traditional Christmas relative is the grim teenager who refuses to participate in the orgy of commercialism and locks himself in his room

Early unsuccessful designs for a Walkman.

with his Hitachi TV, Sony Walkman and Nintendo Gameboy. There is a special time on Christmas day when the head of the family takes it upon himself to make a speech summing up the past year. This time coincides with the rest of the family's sudden desire for fresh air.

REMEMBER: *No Christmas would be complete without bitter old family rivalries and deeply felt animosities being aired. This is called the Queen's Speech.*

You'll know when Christmas is well and truly over when you get a letter from the Royal Mail advising you to post early for Christmas, when your relatives return to their high-security experimental laboratories and when all that is left of your Christmas presents is three bottles of *'Messerschmitt'*.

THE FIVE LEAST WELCOME GUESTS AT CHRISTMAS:

1 The plumber who comes to fix the burst water pipe who, in the best traditions of Christmas spirit, decides to charge only eighty three times his normal emergency call out rate.

2 The parents of the turkey.

3 Anyone who can claim to be related to you but whose name you can't quite recall.

4 Uncle Mike

5 Two gentlemen in Santa Claus hats who have come to repossess your house.

21

SEX

- What do you want for breakfast?
- What on Earth is that?
- Is that enough foreplay?
- Is it safe now?
- Where does this go?

F or the socially ambitious, the bedroom is not somewhere you rest. A true social climber, if they thought it would get them ahead, would merrily sleep their way through the Mormon Tabernacle Choir. There comes a point in flattery when it is no longer enough to add another 'really' to 'You are really, really super'. You have to make the tricky transition to something more physical, which means either playing golf or making love. Base your decision on whether you prefer being embarrassed slipping your trousers on or off.

What do you want for breakfast?

Opening gambits should be appropriate to the height you have attained on the social ladder and should range from *'Shag?'* to *'You know your eyes are the same colour as my Lamborghini'* (not good if for some reason you have a pink Lamborghini). While you're making your play keep a watchful eye on your target's body language. Lots of deep breathing and sweating means full steam ahead. Lying quietly in their best suit, nose hair neatly trimmed, looking pale and peaceful and surrounded by grieving relatives means back off.

Getting people into bed is not as easy as your friends would have you believe. Some people look upon their genitals in the same way as Mrs Thatcher views the Falklands. They unilaterally impose a two hundred mile total exclusion zone around them and then defend them with bewildering ferocity. If this is the case don't bother because, as with the Falklands, once you actually get there, there's not much to write home about. Playing hard-to-get is a time-honoured method of getting other people into bed, but be careful that you don't overdo it.

WARNING: *Play hard-to-get too well and you get exactly the same results as a vow of chastity.*

One leg on the wireless stand was a popular position in the fifties

The rhythm method is another interesting sexual variation. This involves only having sex at a particular time, i.e. every time you want to add another member to your family. This type of sexual behaviour is commonly associated with a particular religious group – Methodists.

What on Earth is that?

The laws of desire are an incredibly difficult and complex mix of chemistry, hormones, atmosphere and other intangibles. Except for men, of course, who have the sexual sophistication of a wing-nut. For men there is only one issue; *'Is size important?'* Unless you're talking about your wallet, the answer you're most likely to get is, *'not if you're worried about it, dear.'* However

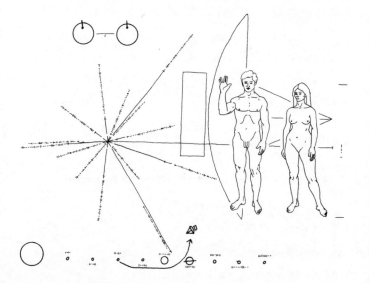

Calculation required to find the 'G-spot'.

there is one sure way of testing whether you are well endowed; If a condom fits snugly without having to unroll it you're not. Either way it's worth remembering that proportionally nothing in the animal kingdom is as well endowed as the slug, and look how far that gets them. For women there is a school of thought that says the key to real pleasure is the G-spot. Sadly the average man has more chance of finding the Holy Grail. Man or woman, the most erotic organ is supposed to be the brain. Don't you believe it. There's nothing romantic about waking up next to a big wet brain.

If women really wanted men to get at their breasts they would have Velcro bra straps instead of an array of hooks and loops that put one in mind of a parlour game for micro surgeons. Prisons would be a lot more secure if they replaced their locks with bra fastenings; Men would never get out, or go mad in the attempt. On the other hand women get a raw deal when it comes to mens' underpants. Men simply can't get it into their heads that women are unlikely to be inspired to remove underpants with their teeth if when they do so they will be eye to eye with a little Noddy motif.

Is that enough foreplay?

Making love is like making tea. For best results you have to warm the pot. Tradition dictates a period of foreplay which consists of giving intimate attention to parts of the body whose only regular visitor is eczema. Foreplay experts recommend light kissing of the whole of your partner's body. If after three hours kissing you've covered less than a third of their total body area, give up, or at least have a cup of tea. Lately a ridiculous fashion has arisen of incorporating food into foreplay.

WARNING: *If you think your partner is likely to insist on this, make sure the contents of your fridge consist of rhubarb crumble, dried apricots and suet. If they can make a go of that lot, then they probably have a background in catering.*

The English gave a vast number of good, healthy clean sports to the world. This was to make up for their sex lives which are very far from healthy. Virtually every perverted form of gratification has its origins in the English upper middle classes, who first come up with the deviation and then make up laws punishing people caught doing it, thus giving themselves double satisfaction. The word fetish itself comes from Captain Stanley Fetish, who rode in the charge of the Light Brigade, dressed from head to foot in a

Barrier contraception methods can be overdone.

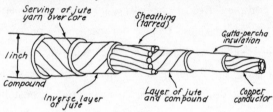

tight rubber bodice. Unfortunately for him he was one of the few to come back alive.

Toe sucking has become rather popular of late and has been sanctioned as a permissible form of procreation by the sexual experts at the Vatican. If you do feel drawn to your partners toes and the sucking thereof, do make sure you check their bathroom cabinets first for any products from Dr Scholl. And remember; never, ever use your teeth.

FIVE SEX TOYS THAT JUST MAKE YOU LOOK BLOODY SILLY:
1   A rubber dinghy that seats twelve
2   A two litre tin of Swarfega
3   An inflatable guinea pig
4   A crash helmet
5   A thick wynciette nightie, decorated with tiny pink bows

Is it safe now?

S afe sex for a social climber is sex with Debrett's in one hand and a banker's reference in the other. Of course condoms also rear their ugly little heads. Once on they leave the male organ with all the sensitivity of a croquet mallet. This is not necessarily a bad thing if you need something for propping doors open or scraping the ice off windscreens. For men condoms do have one redeeming feature in that after the event the excuse of having to get rid of the little horror can be used to escape the incredibly irksome post-coital cuddle.

Drugs and sex have always been intimately associated. Generally this amounts to a couple of aspirin kept handy to tackle the rash of headaches that tend to accompany normal sexual encounters.

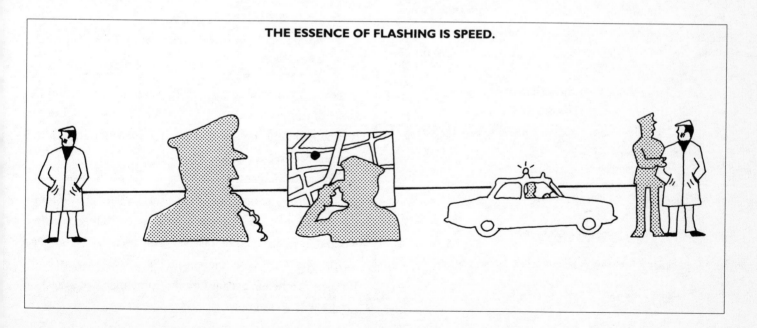

THE ESSENCE OF FLASHING IS SPEED.

Where does this go?

*E*astern civilisation gave the Kama Sutra to the art of making love. Couples who attempt all eighty-seven positions in the Kama Sutra would do well to keep the companion volume with them; Eightly-seven Ways to Deal with Excruciating Cramp. In the Kama Sutra (which translated means 'Watch your Elbow') the various positions have lyrical descriptions such as *'Two dying swans'*. If the author had spent a little more time in bed instead of on the river bank, the positions would have more realistic descriptions such as *'Pig in a*

FIVE THINGS MEN SHOULD AVOID SAYING

AFTER MAKING LOVE:

1 *'What's for dinner?'*

2 *'I hope you didn't mind me cutting it short but I didn't want to miss Final Score'*

3 *'I was right, slim women are better in bed'*

4 *'I enjoyed that so much, I'm going to give up my highly paid job'*

5 *'Will you marry me?'*

FIVE THINGS WOMEN SHOULD AVOID SAYING

AFTER MAKING LOVE:

1 *'Is that it?'*

2 *'Let's do it again, now'*

3 *'Right, that's got your nasty little urges out of the way, let's have a look at those tax papers'*

4 *'The ceiling could do with a lick of paint'*

5 *'My husband is standing in that cupboard where he keeps his shotguns'*

---

wheelbarrow'. Western civilisation's own unique contribution to the art of love is premature ejaculation. If this happens during sex don't worry. If it happens in the restaurant three hours before, worry.

The post-match analysis is the most crucial moment in sex. Short of a team of excited seismologists bursting into the room, men really have no means of telling whether women have enjoyed themselves. Few men ask *'How was it for you?'* in case the answer is *'How was what?'* Women rarely ask because by that time men are asleep or on the way to the pub.

DISCLAIMER

The author asserts his moral right not to be associated with any of the views expressed or not expressed in this or any other work by him or anybody else. All of the characters in this book are fictitious, and any resemblance to actual persons, living, dead or otherwise is deliberately coincidental.

No part of this book is to be copied, reproduced, mimeographed, eaten or used as a prop in fringe theatre productions. This book is not to be read in jails, oil rigs, local council meetings, nor is it to be used during periods of national mourning, mass love-ins or freak electrical storms.

Medical opinion suggests that this book should not be read while driving, during heavy petting or during any form of satanic ritual abuse.

Any person in contravention of any of the above clauses will be fiercely prosecuted by teams of bitter humourless lawyers.